Letting Your Property

London: The Stationery Office

Disclaimer

This book puts YOU in control. That is an excellent thing, but it also makes YOU responsible for using it properly. Few washing machine manufacturers will honour their guarantee if you don't follow their 'instructions for use'. In the same way, we are unable to accept liability for any loss arising from mistakes or misunderstandings on your part. So please take time to read this book carefully.

This book is not a definitive statement of the law, although we believe it to be accurate and up-to-date as of 1 September 2001. We cannot accept liability for changes in the law that take place after the publication date, although every effort will be made to show any such changes on the website.

Contents

About the authors

Mark Fairweather is a practising solicitor, and is one of the founding partners of the legal firm Fairweather Stephenson & Co. He is co-author with Rosy Border of the Stationery Office's *Simply Legal* series of DIY law kits as well as five titles in the *You Need This Book First* series. He has two children and lives in Suffolk.

Rosy Border has a First in French and has worked in publishing, lecturing, journalism and the law. She is a prolific author and adapter who stopped counting after 150 titles. Rosy and her husband, John Rabson, live in an old farmhouse in Suffolk and have a grown-up family. Rosy enjoys entertaining, DIY and retail therapy in French markets.

Welcome

Welcome to the *You Need This Book First* series. Let's face it – the law is a maze. This book is your map through the part of the maze that deals with letting residential property. It contains everything lawyers would tell you about this, if only they had time (and you had the money to pay them). And if you follow our advice you should end up with a tenancy agreement that:

- does what you want it to do
- is legally sound
- you as a non-lawyer can understand.

Acknowledgements

A glance at the *Useful Contacts* section will show how many individuals and organisations helped us to compile this book. Thank you, everyone, and especial thanks to Nigel Pratt, Chartered Accountant, for advice on tax and to John Rabson, Chartered Engineer, for IT support, research and refreshments.

Introduction

This book

- provides the general information that professional advisers would give you on the subject, if only they had the time, and if only you had the money to pay them

- tells you the buzzwords that are important in this section of the law, and what they mean

- provides samples of the letters, etc., you need

- answers some of the most frequently asked questions on the subject

- is supported by a website that is regularly updated.

Although our book gives you, as landlord, the fullest protection the law can offer, combined with a fair deal for your tenant, we cannot guarantee that everything will go perfectly all the time. There will always be bad tenants, tenants who are slow payers, tenants who damage their landlord's property or fall out with the neighbours. A bad tenant could cost you a lot of money as well as a great deal of stress. Our book minimises the risks for you by:

- advising you about choosing your tenant;

- advising you about vetting your tenant;

- making your tenant legally responsible for paying the rent and looking after your property;

- making sure you can get your tenant out when you want to;

- offering general advice on tax, mortgage and insurance considerations.

This book empowers you. That is a good thing; but it means responsibility as well as power. Think of yourself as a driver using a road map. The map tells you the route, but it is up to you to drive carefully. Watch out for the road signs along the route.

Hazard signs

We tell you when you are in danger of getting out of your depth and need to take professional advice. Watch out for the hazard signs.

Legal lore

Sometimes we pause to explain something: the origin of a word, perhaps, or why a particular piece of legislation was passed. You do not need to know these things to make use of this book, but we hope you find them interesting.

Power points

Sometimes we pause to empower you to do something.
Watch out for the symbol.

Clear English rules OK

We draft WYSIWYG documents – *w*hat *y*ou *s*ee *i*s *w*hat
*y*ou *g*et.

Legal documents have traditionally been written in
archaic language, because this wording has stood the
test of time – often several centuries – and has been
hallowed by the courts. What is more, the use of
technical language can sometimes enable specialists to
express esoteric concepts in a kind of professional
shorthand that is useful to them but meaningless to
others.

The use of archaic language is, however, unnecessary
and may be dangerous. The worst problem is that for
non-specialists it is a foreign language, unknown at
worst and incompletely understood at best, with all the
potential for misunderstanding which that entails.

Why write tenancy agreements in a foreign language in
preference to plain English? What is important is that it
is legally sound and is expressed in clear, unambiguous
language that accurately reflects your intentions.

On the (fairly rare) occasions when we *do* need to use
technical language, we offer clear explanations (see
Buzzwords on page 5).

We're on the web

Check out our website, because buying this book gives you the right to use our exclusive readers' website.

www.youneedthisfirst.co.uk

Buzzwords

assured shorthold tenancy (AST) – a popular way of renting property in the private sector.

Tenancy means living in someone's property in exchange for rent. *Assured* in this context means the tenancy is subject to the statutory framework of housing legislation. And *shorthold* means short term – well, short by some standards: the minimum period is in effect six months.

buy-to-let mortgages – loans to enable people to borrow money to buy property to rent out; the idea – in theory at least – is that the rent from the property covers the monthly payments on the loan and the potential rental income is taken into account when the lender assesses the borrower's ability to service the loan.

company let – a situation where a tenancy is taken on by a company rather than by an individual. See page 64 for the pros and cons of this arrangement.

deposit – a sum of money which the tenant hands the landlord at the start of a tenancy, to cover any unpaid rent, to pay the cost of cleaning the property when the tenant leaves and to make good any damage the tenant has done. The landlord holds the deposit and returns it (less any such deductions) to the tenant at the end of the letting period.

discretionary – a matter of free choice (unfortunately, not usually *your* choice); the opposite of *mandatory*.

exclusive possession – a tenant's right to occupy the property they rent and be able to lock out the rest of the world, apart from (arranged) visits for inspection, maintenance, etc. It is exclusive possession that distinguishes a *tenancy* (see below), where the tenant does have exclusive possession, from a *licence* (see below), where a resident landlord or landlady can come and go at will in the premises the licensee occupies.

freehold – property ownership in which you own the property for ever – unless you sell it, of course. There is no time limit, as there is with a lease. One other feature is that freeholders hardly ever pay rent.

ground rent – a nominal rent paid by flat owners – to the owner of the building (often called the *head landlord* or *ground rent landlord*) of which the flat forms part. Flat owners will often also pay a service charge, which is usually far from nominal!

habitable – fit to be lived in.

initial period – the fixed time for which a property is let on an AST (see above), after which, if both landlord and tenant agree, the property can be let for another fixed period or on a week-to-week or month-to-month basis.

inventory – a room-by-room list of the contents of a property and its condition at the time of letting.

The landlord and tenant go through the inventory together at the beginning of the tenancy to check that everything is there. Both sign it, and at the end of the tenancy they go through the inventory again.

jointly and severally – (as in *jointly and severally responsible/liable*) together and individually. Think of *severing* into several separate bits.

If two or more tenants sign the tenancy agreement, they are *jointly and severally* responsible for the rent and *jointly and severally* liable for any damage. This means that the full amount can be claimed from any or from all of them.

landlord – someone to whom a tenant pays rent in return for a tenancy in accommodation owned by the landlord.

Legal lore

Land comes from the Old English for a strip of field and looms large in the legal consciousness.

lease – a legal interest in land; in this context, a contract between landlord and tenant giving the tenant exclusive possession (see above), for a definable limited period, of property owned by the landlord, almost invariably in exchange for rent. A lease is essentially the same as a *tenancy* (see below).

leasehold – the form of property ownership which is limited in time (eg 6 months, 999 years) and is characterised by payment of rent to a landlord. Flats are usually leasehold. All tenancy agreements are forms of leasehold.

If you own a leasehold flat, you will have to pay ground rent to the ground rent landlord. At the end of the lease, in 99 or 999 years or whatever, the flat will revert to the landlord. For that reason, a lease is often referred to as a 'wasting asset'.

licence – a personal right to occupy property, but without rights of *exclusive possession* (see above). The commonest kind of licence is the arrangement between a resident landlord and a lodger or *licensee*, who typically has their own room and shares some facilities with the landlord.

mandatory – compulsory, the opposite of *discretionary.*

notice – a formal announcement that you are going to do something, such as leave a property or repossess it.

reference – a statement about the character and (sometimes) creditworthiness of a prospective tenant.

resident landlord – this is a landlord who lives in the same premises as their tenant/lodger. If you are a resident landlord you need the book *Taking in a Lodger* in this series.

self-contained – a complete unit, not sharing any facilities.

statutory – fixed by law (statute).

sub-letting – the letting by a flat owner or other tenant of all or part of the property that they rent.

ten per cent wear and tear – the standard figure allowed by the Inland Revenue in respect of annual upkeep of rental property. If your annual receipts from rent come to £3,000, you are allowed £300 a year towards maintenance even if (chance would be a fine thing!) you do not in fact spend that amount; and you do not have to say in detail how you spent the money. See page 111 for a fuller explanation.

tenancy – a typical lawspeak definition is 'an arrangement under which exclusive possession of a property is granted for a fixed or ascertainable period of time' – almost invariably in return for rent.

There are two key elements here: the 'exclusive possession' (see above) and the 'ascertainable period of time'. The tenancy agreement has to say *when* the tenancy is to start and *when* (or how, eg 'two months' notice') it is to end. During that 'ascertainable period of time' the tenant enjoys exclusive use of the property, as opposed to a lodger who does not. Tenants have more legal protection than lodgers.

Frequently asked questions

—I want to let my house for a year while I am working abroad. How can I be sure of getting my tenant out when I come home?

Grant them an assured shorthold tenancy (see *Buzzwords*). We show you how.

—I want to let my house for a month while I am working abroad. How can I be sure of getting my tenant out when I come home?

One month – no can do (see below).

—I want to let my house for two months while I am working abroad. How can I be sure of getting my tenant out when I come home?

The short answer is, think carefully. Is it worth it?

The long answer is that you cannot use an AST because it does not give you the right to take back the property from your tenant until a minimum of six months has passed. You can still let your house for two months, but first the tenancy must not be shorthold, and second, you must serve written notice on the tenant – before the tenancy starts – that you have occupied the property as your only or principal home. The notice should make reference to Ground 1 Part 1 Schedule 2 of the Housing

Act 1988. If the tenant then refuses to move out, you have to serve another notice on them – a Section 8 notice – asking for possession. The wording of the Section 8 notice is prescribed by law (creativity is not encouraged), and in any case must allow the tenant a further two months to leave. So, if you serve your Ground 1 and Section 8 notices at the same time, you can in theory limit the tenancy to two months. If the tenant digs their heels in, you can apply to the court for possession. There is a quickie procedure (see page 109) using Form N5A, but realistically you will need to allow another two months – and if the tenant still won't go, you will need to instruct the court bailiffs to remove your tenant – another two months. Is it, cosmically, worth your while?

I have a mortgage on my property. Am I allowed to let it?

Almost certainly, but you must first get your mortgage lender's agreement. Some mortgage lenders extort an annual fee for the paperwork they say this involves them in. Up to £100 is usual, and they add it to your mortgage, so you don't have any choice in the matter. The lender may also increase the interest rate – in which case, consider moving to a different mortgage lender. Take care, however, to ensure that the new loan attracts tax relief. This is not a DIY matter. Seek professional advice to avoid making a saving in one area and wasting money in another.

— **Does a tenancy have to be for a fixed period, or can it run indefinitely?**

Both are possible. You can have a fixed term tenancy, which lasts for a fixed number of weeks, months or years, or a periodic tenancy, which runs indefinitely from one rent period to the next. In practice, when the initial fixed period of an AST has passed, the letting can continue as a periodic tenancy for as long as it suits both landlord and tenant.

 — **I own a flat in a 99-year lease. Can I rent it out?**

Yes, provided your lease allows you to do so. If in doubt, check with your ground rent landlord (see *Buzzwords*). You should also check with the building insurer to make sure the policy covers letting – and, separately, your contents insurers (see *Are you insured?* on page 45).

 — **Do I need to instruct a solicitor to draw up an assured shorthold tenancy agreement?**

No. If you follow our instructions carefully you will end up with a legally sound AST.

 — **My house is owned by a housing association. I shall be working in Wales for a year and would like to sublet my home. Is this allowed?**

Probably; it depends on the terms of your lease. You will almost certainly need to ask your housing association's permission, and you should also check with the building insurer (and your contents insurer)

that the property would be covered during the letting
(see page 45 for further details).

**I have been told that if I let an unfurnished
property, it is harder to get tenants out than if I let
it furnished. Is this so?** ——————————————

Not any more. For many years there has been no
distinction between furnished and unfurnished
property from the point of view of ease of eviction.
Today, it is the kind of tenancy granted, not the
furniture, which governs this. Our AST agreement
applies to both furnished and unfurnished property.

**Can I charge a deposit, and what would be a
reasonable amount?** —————————————————

Yes, you can; and one month's rent would be quite
normal. Do not charge more than two month's rent.
Read about deposits on pages 90–92.

Do I need to provide a rent book? —————————

Only if the rent is payable on a weekly basis. You must,
however, keep a record of all rent payments. It is also a
good idea to provide receipts to avoid disagreements
later.

**Who is responsible for repairing 'baths, bogs,
boilers and basins' – my tenant or me?** ——————

You are. You are responsible for the fabric of the
building, heating and hot water installations (unless, of
course, it was your tenant who did the damage). See
page 33 for details.

—**I have inherited my late father's house and I would like to rent it out; but I am worried about paying a lot of tax. Can you advise?**

Without knowing your precise details, no. The general rule is that you will pay tax if, after deducting your expenses, your letting income comes to more than your personal tax allowances. There is general advice on tax on page 110 of this book. The smart thing to do, however, is to visit the Inland Revenue website (see *Useful Contacts* on page 163) and pick up all the free literature you can. Alternatively, seek professional advice.

—**Do I need to instruct a letting agent?**

No. Many landlords do it themselves, although it is sensible to instruct an agent if, for example, you will be out of the country or frantically busy. We tell you the pros and cons of DIY or agent on pages 54–61.

—**If I sell a rental property and make a profit, shall I have to pay Capital Gains Tax?**

Yes, unless the capital profit is small, or relief and exemptions apply. The annual exemption for individuals is currently £7,500. The other main relief is taper relief – the concept being that the longer you own the asset, the lower the rate of tax.

Moreover, if the letting has been short term and the rental property is your main or only home, you may qualify for Private Residence Relief. Call your local

Inland Revenue office and ask for leaflet CGT1 and
help sheet IR283.

What records will I have to keep?

For the Inland Revenue, you must keep details of rents
received and money paid out in respect of the rental
property. You have to keep this information for six
years after the tax year in question. See *Record keeping*
on page 101.

What rights of access to my rental property do I have as landlord?

You, or anyone acting for you (eg a workman), have
only whatever rights your tenancy agreement gives you.
Usually a tenancy agreement will give you the right to
enter the property at reasonable times of day to do any
repairs that are your responsibility, and also to inspect
the property. You will usually be required to give
24 hours' notice of any inspection. All this is set out in
the sample tenancy agreement on page 120. Note that
entering the property without the right to do so, or
without giving notice, may amount to harassment.

I read somewhere that I had to have a deed in order to rent out my property. Is this right?

No – unless the agreement is for a fixed period of
three years or more.

—**Can the tenant challenge the rent?**

Yes, the tenant can make a one-time-only application to the local Rent Assessment Committee (details in your local phone book) within the first 6 months of the tenancy – after that it's too late. The Committee can adjust the rent to bring it into line with market rates.

After the initial fixed period of the tenancy, *you* can apply to the Committee (ask them for the official form to do this) if you want to increase the rent and the tenant does not agree the amount you want.

You are
making history

From the earliest times until the end of the First World War, almost everybody, even the very rich, rented his or her home. Remember Jane Austen's *Pride and Prejudice*:

> *'My dear Mr Bennet', said his lady to him one day, 'have you heard that Netherfield Park is let at last?... a young man of large fortune from the north of England'.*

And Anne Brontë did not name her novel *The Owner of Wildfell Hall.*

In the days when most homes were rented from private landlords (for local authority housing is a recent development – see below), the landlord could be your guardian angel – such as the great philanthropists Titus Salt and Robert Owen – or a bogeyman (when you are tired of 19th century novelists, dip into Catherine Cookson's *The Dwelling Place*) to his tenants. When the landlord was also the farmer, mine owner or factory owner and the house went with the job, the death or dismissal of the breadwinner could make the whole family homeless.

After the First World War 'social housing' became common. Local authorities built low-rent housing for people who could not afford to buy their own homes. The tenants of a local authority had much more security than the tenants of a private landlord had. It was a lot harder for a local authority to evict anyone, for example, than for a rascally landlord who could just send the boys round and change the locks (see *A new word,* below).

Council houses routinely offered modern conveniences – flush lavatories, running water, electricity and so on – which privately rented homes did not. People moved gratefully into three-bedroom semis with little gardens back and front, or bright, cheerful council flats with their own bathrooms. And the council, unlike very many private landlords, took care of all the repairs.

Private landlords' failure to maintain their property satisfactorily was not always a matter of callous indifference. In many cases the money was simply not available. Councils could put up the rates to finance repairs, so that the whole private and business population subsidised the council tenants. Private landlords did not have this option. You can't get blood out of a stone and the rental income of a property regularly fell short of the cost of maintaining and repairing it. Even good landlords, therefore, could find themselves unable to supply their tenants with decent accommodation.

While local authorities were doing their bit for the housing shortage, a number of individuals and groups were also getting in on the act. Prince Albert had started a trend in the 19th century with his 'Model

Artisan's Dwelling House' and a number of wealthy
philanthropists followed suit in providing decent,
affordable accommodation for the 'deserving poor'.
Fine – they had income from other sources ...

A new word

And so public and private landlords coexisted, not
always harmoniously. Then, in the 1950s, a Polish
immigrant called Peter Rachman took advantage of the
wave of West Indians who were invited to come to
Britain to work. Rachman bought up hundreds of slum
properties in Notting Hill and Bayswater for derisory
sums and let them to West Indians. Prejudice and
discrimination (there was no racial equality legislation
in those days) meant the new arrivals could not get any
other place to live. Rachman welcomed them all. He
also bullied, molested, overcharged and overcrowded
his tenants and subjected them to a reign of terror.
There were no laws to protect them from Rachman and
his bully boys; and they had nowhere else to go.

Rachman died of a heart attack in his early forties, but
not before his name had entered the English language,
alongside Mr Guillotin's beheading device and
Mr Biro's pen. New laws were passed to protect tenants
from mistreatment, but not before *Rachmanism* –
defined in the OED as 'exploitation of slum tenants by
unscrupulous landlords' – had entered our language.

The decline of the private landlord

And so, fuelled in part by the Rachman scandal, legislation was enacted.

Landlords no longer had the right to turn their tenants out into the howling gale in a fit of pique. And tenants were given the right, if they felt that their rent was too high, or that the landlord was not maintaining the property adequately, to apply for a 'fair rent' or an order for the landlord to carry out repairs.

The trouble about a 'fair rent' was that it was usually a lot lower than the going rate in that area and that meant less money available for repairs than ever before. At the same time, many tenants became *regulated or controlled* tenants. The practical effect of this was that their landlords could neither evict them nor raise their rents. As late as the 1980s there were people who were paying only a few pounds a week to rent property that, if only their landlord could sell it with vacant possession, would fetch hundreds of thousands of pounds. Empty, the property was worth a fortune: tenanted, it was unsaleable.

What we are looking at here is a shift in the balance of power. Where once the system favoured the private landlord, often to a quite grotesque extent, by the 1960s landlords were desperate to get rid of their tenanted accommodation for whatever it would fetch. This was done simply to shed the burden of property which brought them no income and which they could not afford to maintain.

Gradually the pool of property available for ordinary private rental dried up, until the only properties offered were the pits: damp, unmodernised and deeply unattractive.

You can't really blame the landlords. Would you want to be responsible for property that you could not afford to repair, with no chance of evicting bad tenants or getting a reasonable rent?

At the same time, with cheap mortgages that attracted tax relief, more and more ordinary people were buying their own homes. By 1990 only 7% of housing in Britain was privately rented; the other 93% was either local authority/housing association property or privately owned (usually with a mortgage).

A few landlords found a way around the problem by granting 'holiday lets' for a month at a time, although in practice they could be renewed almost indefinitely. This was against the law, but there was such a dire shortage of rental accommodation that the law did not want to know.

The rise of the letting agent

There were two other kinds of landlord, however. First, there was Mr Relocation. Typically, Mr Relocation had landed a well paid short-term contract a long way from home and needed to let his home in Britain for a year or so to finance accommodation near his new place of work. Homes like this tended to be very desirable. Their owners were naturally choosy about whom they let them to, and anxious to be able to move into their homes again when their work contract ended.

The second kind of landlord was less fortunate. Mr and Mrs Mobile also needed to move house to be near Mr Mobile's new job, but they were moving permanently, not on a short-term basis like Mr Relocation. They had bought their home at a time when house prices were high. Falling house prices (remember the recession in the late 1980s?) meant that the Mobiles owed more to their mortgage lender than their house was currently worth. So they were unable to do what they wanted, which was sell their existing home to finance the purchase of a similar property in the new location. This is 'negative equity', and it was a nightmare, because if you did sell your home you would still owe the mortgage lender many thousands of pounds.

There was only one way out, and that was to let this unsaleable property until house prices rose again, and meanwhile possibly rent somewhere in a new location.

In response to these needs, a new life form evolved – the letting agent – and soon a new 'professional body' – the Association of Residential Letting Agents (see *Useful Contacts*) – was set up to advise them. The landlords supplied the property and the agents accepted the responsibility of managing it, often charging both landlord and tenant for doing so.

The assured shorthold tenancy

'It's renting, but not as we know it' is one of the many things Captain Kirk of the Starship *Enterprise* never said.

The Housing Act 1988 became law in January 1989 and turned the whole private rental sector upside down. The Act aimed to give both landlords and tenants a fairer deal, and to make more properties available for rent. It introduced a new and attractive concept: a legally binding agreement which allowed properties to be rented for short bursts, typically six months at a time. There were five good things about the new tenancy from the landlord's point of view:

- the landlord could charge a market rent;

- the agreement committed the tenant to pay the rent for the whole of the six months even if they did not stay the full time;

- after the initial period of six months, the tenant could stay on for another fixed term or for an indefinite period that could be terminated by two months' notice from the landlord, and whatever notice period the agreement required from the tenant.

- the landlord was sure of getting the tenant out; even if a tenant refused to budge and a court order was needed to get them out, the court would have to grant the order provided the paperwork was correct;

- rent increases could be imposed after the first year, although no more than one increase in any 12-month period.

Landlords realised that they would no longer be stuck with either artificially low rents or with unevictable tenants, and responded favourably. And safety regulations were now in force which have probably made Rachman turn in his grave but have probably saved many lives. You can read about these regulations in *Is your property habitable?* on page 32.

The law relating to ASTs was amended by the Housing Act 1996. The main effects of the 1996 Act are:

- an AST is the default form of residential tenancy. Unless the tenancy is a continuation of a previous letting, which was not an AST, or you agree with your tenant that the letting will not be an AST, or it is a form of letting which cannot be an AST (eg a holiday let or lodger agreement), it will be an AST by default;

- there is no longer a minimum six-month period of letting, but unless the tenant has broken the terms of the tenancy the landlord cannot repossess the property for six months anyway;

- although an AST agreement can be made orally (unwise!), the tenant is entitled to a written statement of the principal terms.

Letting for profit

A new breed of landlord has evolved in recent years, thanks in some part to the belief (misguided or otherwise!) that property increases in value in the long term, and thanks also to the buy-to-let scheme. This scheme was dreamed up by the ARLA and a group of sympathetic mortgage lenders.

Previously it was difficult to borrow money to buy property to rent out because mortgage lenders favoured owner-occupiers, and other lenders (such as banks) charged high interest. It seemed to be considered immoral to borrow money to buy rental property. Even renting out your own home, if it was mortgaged, required the lender's special permission. Buy-to-let is different. It is intended specifically to enable people to buy property to let. In fact, you aren't supposed to live in a buy-to-let financed property yourself. There is more about buy-to-let on page 48.

Modern landlords – and modern tenants

There are rascally landlords still lurking in the darker corners of the private rented sector, but most private landlords nowadays are decent people who would not turn a family out in the snow even if the law allowed them to.

Some own several properties, all bought for cash in a down-at-heel state, which they have renovated and equipped to a high standard: 'I never had a doll's house as a child; this is the grown-up version'.

Some see bricks and mortar as a surer long-term investment than stocks and shares: 'My properties are my pension fund'.

Whatever their motives, landlords like these are doing a good job – and adding to the pool of property for rent.

At the same time, different people are choosing to rent.

For a time there seemed to be a stigma attached to renting. When council tenants were given the right to buy their homes, often at very low prices, the percentage of owner-occupiers rocketed. Anyone who was anybody, or aspired to be anybody, scraped a deposit together to 'own' their home, even if in reality all they owned was a huge millstone of debt and the doubtful privilege of repairing their own roof and rodding their own drains. But times change. As WS Gilbert says, 'When everyone is Somebody, Then no one's Anybody', ... and so renting became socially acceptable again.

We are not sure if official statistics will bear this out, but we have the impression that with the rise in marriage break-ups there are a great many people from all walks of life looking for property to rent. If your marriage has gone sour and your ex is living in the former family home with the children, you may not have the wherewithal to get on the housing ladder again; and you may not want the responsibility of home ownership, because you are not sure of your long-term plans. So you rent.

Then there are the professionals. The young single ones rent something smart and clean and labour-saving because, although they could afford to buy, they do not want the chores or the long-term commitment; and they do not see why they should put down a four figure sum as a deposit on something which may turn out to be in the wrong place. They'd rather have a car.

Or a family man lands his dream job, a long way from home. He doesn't want to uproot his family; they are doing just fine where they are. So he rents somewhere near his work and goes home to his family at weekends. His only outlay is the deposit on his rented property, and that is returnable.

ASTs suit all these 'new tenants' perfectly. Are *you* ready to be a 'new landlord'?

Before you let your property

Are you a resident or a non-resident landlord?

We need to ask this question before you go any further, because the answer will govern whether this book is in fact for you!

All residential tenancies are subject to statutory control. That means that you do not have complete freedom to agree anything you like with your tenant. The legal framework is, however, different for tenants on the one hand and lodgers on the other. You need to establish which party you are at.

Answer the questions below.

1. *Do you live somewhere other than the property you are letting?*

If the answer is yes, you are a non-resident landlord, and the AST agreement that can be found on page 121 is for you.

2. *Is the accommodation you are planning to let self-contained, even if you live under the same roof?*

28

If the answer is yes, you are still a non-resident landlord and the AST agreement that can be found on page 120 is for you too.

3. *Do you plan to let rooms in your home with shared facilities?*

If so, you are a resident landlord and you're at the wrong party – see our *Taking in a Lodger* book in the same series.

The assured shorthold tenancy explained

What does this mean in plain English? Well, 'tenancy' means living in someone's property in exchange for rent. 'Assured' means the tenancy is subject to the statutory framework of housing legislation. 'Shorthold' means short term – but see below on what this really means. Here's how an AST works:

1. Unless the tenant has broken the terms of the tenancy the landlord cannot repossess the property for six months.

In practice, most ASTs start with an initial fixed period. There is no upper limit, but six months to one year would be normal. There is a balance here between flexibility and security of income. If, however, you grant the tenancy for more than, say, 12 months, make sure you include the right to review the rent.

After the fixed term – the six months, year or whatever – you can either renew the letting for another fixed period or allow the letting to continue indefinitely on a periodic basis (usually month to month). If you are renewing for a fixed period you will need a fresh tenancy agreement. Otherwise you do not need to take any action to continue the letting, apart from making the tenant aware that you are continuing on the same terms as the original letting except that you are no longer talking about a fixed term. To end the letting, follow the advice in *Getting 'em out* on page 104.

2. The tenant is responsible for paying the rent for the whole of the initial period even if they leave early. (In practice if you find a replacement you may decide to let them off the hook, but it is not obligatory.)

3. You can grant an AST which does not have an initial fixed period – but remember that unless the tenant breaks the terms of the tenancy, you cannot repossess the property for six months anyway.

4. If your proposed tenant is already living in property owned by you on some basis other than an AST, it may not be possible for you to grant them one. If this applies to you, please take expert advice.

5. If the rent you are charging is higher than the going rate for comparable property in your area, your tenant can apply to a Rent Assessment Committee for the rent to be reduced in line with the going rate. It is, however, open to you to take steps to terminate the tenancy at the earliest opportunity, but in general this cannot be earlier than the date when your fixed term ends.

6. You cannot make your tenant leave until the end of the initial period at the very earliest, unless your tenant has failed to keep their side of the bargain. To repossess your property, you must give the tenant a statutory notice, the 'Notice of Intention to Apply for Possession' that is on page 156 of this book. Unless you are seeking possession because the tenant is at fault, you will not be entitled to have your property back until at least two months after the tenant has received your notice (there is more about this on page 106).

7. If the tenant refuses to move out you must get a court order to take back your property. Do not try removing them by force without a court order: that is a criminal offence. So is harassing your tenant. If you do evict your tenant unlawfully, you can be made to pay substantial compensation.

Legal lore

Harassment can take many forms. Here are just a few examples of hostile acts by landlords that have fallen foul of the Protection from Eviction Act 1977.

- kicking the tenant's door every time they went past;
- sabotaging the hot water supply or blocking the lavatory;
- turning off the gas, electricity or water without good cause;

- removing slates from the roof;

- taking up floorboards every weekend on the pretext of repairing the electric wiring.

(Rachman, thou shouldst be living at this hour …)
An AST means you can get 'em out when their time is up without sending the boys round. Even if your tenants dig their heels in and refuse to budge, the court *must* find in your favour provided you have got your paperwork right. So you can skip the sabotage.

Is your property habitable?

As landlord of a residential property, you have a statutory duty (a duty which you cannot dodge, even if your tenant is on your side) to provide your tenant with accommodation which is:

- safe;

- habitable;

- free from serious disrepair.

Nor can you turn a blind eye to these issues; you can be made criminally liable for unsafe property even if you are not aware of the hazards.

To sum up, there must be no leaky roofs, damp, moss or mould; no mice, deathwatch beetles or cockroaches; no impromptu firework displays from dodgy wiring or smells from dodgy gas mains; and there must be adequate washing and toilet facilities and the plumbing must be in good working order: no blockages, leaks or stagnant puddles. And, most importantly, there must be proper fire precautions.

In more detail, this means:

1. The property must be weatherproof and free from damp.

This may sound daunting and possibly expensive, but you might qualify for help in the form of a local authority or central government grant. See *A word on grants* on pages 43–45.

2. It must be free from vermin and insect infestation.

Don't laugh – we know a landlord who bought a house where several flea-ridden cats had lived. The previous owner kindly left the carpets behind. Fleas can live a long time without food and the tenants suffered bitten ankles. The moral is, do not assume that your property is free from infestation – get it checked by your local council. Some charge for their services, others do it free.

3. The electrical wiring must be safe, and so must all of the electrical appliances.

The Landlord and Tenant Act 1985 requires you to ensure that the electrical installation is safe when the tenancy begins, and that it is kept that way throughout the tenancy.

Appliances (as opposed to fixed installations) come under the Electrical Equipment (Safety) Regulations 1994. It is an offence not only to sell dodgy electrical appliances (that is why you so seldom see old toasters in charity shops nowadays) but also to let property containing such items.

Surprisingly, although you have this legal duty to ensure your rental property is electrically safe, there is no compulsory scheme along the lines of the gas safety one (see below). Do not, however, wait for legislation to catch up with common sense. You should have your property checked for electrical safety before you let it, and at regular intervals afterwards. This includes:

● wiring circuits and sockets; and
● all electrical appliances.

The Institution of Electrical Engineers recommends the following test intervals:

● fixed electrical installations – five years;
● household appliances – visual check every six months; full inspection every twelve months.

There are over 2,000 electric shock accidents and over 9,000 electrical fires in homes in the UK every year. From Trading Standards, here is a checklist of electrical safety hazards, any one of which could injure or even kill someone:

- frayed or damaged cables;
- old appliances with metal parts and no earth;
- electric fires with fireguards whose openings are too wide (more than 25 x 12 mm or 50 x 20 mm for silicon-covered elements);
- installations with damage allowing access to live parts (eg damaged plugs);
- lamp sockets with no shielding for the metal part of the bulb;
- loose or worn connectors (eg kettle sockets);
- evidence of overheating;
- wires disconnected;
- wrong fuses used;
- old type wiring (red, green and black instead of the modern brown, blue and green/yellow stripes);
- incorrect plugs or non-working cord grips.

This is a horrifying list. Any one of these electrical faults could start a fire.

You may already know a reliable electrician. If not, the National Inspection Council for Electrical Installation Contractors (details in *Useful Contacts* on page 159), approves electrical contractors who issue detailed electrical safety reports and, if any remedial work is done, provide signed certificates. At the time of writing, a few university accommodation officers are already insisting on electrical safety certificates.

— You may be able to arrange an electrical safety check free of charge. Contact your own electricity supplier in the first instance (there should be a display ad in your local telephone directory). They should be able to give you a freephone number to call.

 — Beware of tenants who bring dodgy electrical equipment into your property. The cautious approach is to supply your own appliances – and make sure they are listed in your inventory.

4. If there is gas, the supply must be safe.

Carbon monoxide gas from poorly installed or badly maintained gas appliances and flues kills about 30 people every year. As a landlord you are responsible for the safety of your tenants. You have a responsibility under the Gas Safety (Installation and Use) Regulations 1998 to have all gas appliances, flues and other fittings checked to make sure they are safe and working satisfactorily. These checks must be carried out not less than every 12 months, and checking isn't enough – you *must* have any repair work or servicing done that the installer says is needed.

You have a duty to make sure that:

● gas fittings (appliances and pipe work) and flues are maintained in a safe condition;

● all installation, maintenance and safety checks must be carried out by a CORGI-registered gas installer;

- a CORGI-registered gas installer must carry out an annual safety check on every gas appliance (nobody else will do);

- a record of each safety check is kept for two years;

- a copy of the current safety check record must be issued to each tenant within 28 days of the check being completed, or to each new tenant before they move in.

The statutory maintenance and safety requirements do not apply to appliances owned by your tenant, nor to flues or chimneys solely connected to appliances owned by your tenant. All the same, it is sensible to get those checked too in case your tenant sets fire to your property or tries to blame any disasters on you.

Checks must have taken place within a year of the start of the tenancy, unless the appliances are less than a year old, in which case they must be inspected within 12 months of their installation date. When your CORGI installer has given your gas installations the all clear, you will be given two copies of a gas safety certificate, one for you and one for your tenant. Keep your copy on file and pass the other to your tenant within 28 days (see above).

—Checking your gas installations is not a DIY job. You *must* call in a CORGI (Council for Registered Gas Installers) installer (see *Useful Contacts* on page 159).

Ensuring gas safety is not a job you can delegate to your tenant! The responsibility is yours alone. Failure to comply with the regulations could land you in court, facing a fine of up to £5,000. And if someone is killed or injured as a result of your negligence in this respect, you could face an unlimited fine or even prison.

—Always note in your diary the date when your gas safety certificate falls due for renewal. It is all too easy to let it lapse, and this would mean breaking the law.

5. There must be a water supply and effective drainage.

6. There must be cooking facilities, including a sink with hot and cold water.

7. There must be access to a wash basin, bath (or shower) and lavatory.

8. There must be adequate heating, lighting and ventilation.

9. Flats and bedsits must have adequate means of escape in case of fire.

You also have a statutory duty to provide smoke
detectors, with fresh batteries. The watchwords here are
Smoke Detectors Act 1991.

Whatever type of residential property you let, you
should consider asking your local fire prevention
officer (whose number will be in your local telephone
directory) to check it out for fire safety. This service
will normally be available free of charge. Take careful
note of the FPO's findings and and act on them. A fire
blanket by the kitchen stove and a smoke alarm on the
landing cost very little – some local fire departments
even provide them free of charge – and could save lives.

10. Upholstered furniture, such as sofas, must be flame-retardant.

The law (Furniture and Furnishings (Fire) (Safety)
Regulations 1988 as amended 1993) requires that all
furniture in any property rented to *new* tenants after
1 January 1997 must comply with the regulations. Since
1988 all new upholstered furniture has had to pass
exacting safety tests, and since 1993 the requirements
were extended to apply to *second-hand* furniture; but
there is still a lot of 'illegal' furniture about, made from
untreated polyurethane foam, which catches fire very
easily and gives off poisonous fumes.

You can have as much flammable furniture as you like
in your own home, but you will be breaking the law
unless the soft furnishings in your rental
accommodation are flame retardant. Turn the item

upside down and look for the label. A typical label will say something along the lines of 'Carelessness causes fire' and has a batch number. If the furniture was manufactured before 1988 it is most unlikely to comply with the regulations.

These labels are usually sewn in. We know an old landlady who cut off all the fire safety labels with her scissors because she thought they spoilt the look of her furniture. Silly – how could she prove that her furniture complied with the law?

Interestingly, there are gaps in this legislation. Although the regulations cover beds, headboards, mattresses, sofa beds, futons, cushions and pillows as well as upholstered furniture, they make no mention of curtains, bedding including duvets, curtains or carpets.

There is a free leaflet available from the DTI. The title is *A Guide to the Furniture and Furnishings (Fire) (Safety) Regulations*. Order it from the Publications Orderline (see *Useful Contacts* on page 162).

If you are doubtful whether any of the furniture in your rental property complies with the regulations, your local Trading Standards Department should be able to advise.

Risk management

You are probably well aware that more accidents happen in the home than anywhere else. Try to minimise the accident potential of the property you propose to let. The buzzword is risk management. Go around your property checking for possible hazards such as:

- dodgy window catches;
- loose bits of carpet, especially on stairs;
- trailing cables;
- splinters in wooden surfaces;
- loose floorboards.

Make a record of your inspection and note any action taken. If you have serious doubts about whether your property meets current standards of fitness and/or safety, your local housing authority may inspect it for you. Local authorities want property to be available for letting in their district and most are happy to do this free of charge.

Having made sure your property is safe, habitable and in good repair, you must also keep the property that way throughout the tenancy (unless, of course, the damage is caused by the tenant).

Your tenant has a responsibility too, of course, to use your property in a responsible way. For instance, if they are going away in winter they should turn off the water

to avoid possible burst pipes. They should unblock the
sink when it gets clogged up. They should not damage
your property, or let anyone else do so.

Suppose your tenant tries to withhold rent because you
are slow in carrying out repairs? This is not allowed.
You can take them to court for rent arrears, or even
evict them after serving the proper notice (see
page 104). The sensible thing, if your tenant is anxious
to get the repairs done quickly, is for them to agree to
get the work done and deduct the cost from the rent,
passing the receipted invoices to you. But this is
something you must decide between you – a tenant who
goes ahead without getting your agreement is out of
order.

What if a tenant tries a spot of DIY repair work and
gets it wrong? The law says they must put things right
or pay for someone else to do so.

—Don't let all this worry you. The letting agreement
reproduced in this book sets out the rights and duties of
both you and your tenant.

Optional items

You do NOT, however, have a statutory duty to provide
furniture, carpets or curtains even for a 'furnished'
property. Believe it or not, all those things are optional
items to be agreed between you and your tenant.

'Unfit' property

If you let 'unfit' property – property that does not meet——
the statutory requirements – you can get into serious
trouble. If the worst happens and someone dies or is
injured, you can be sued. Meanwhile, the local
authority, your tenant or both of them together can
compel you to carry out remedial work. You may
receive a *repair notice* to carry out repairs to make your
property fit for human habitation, or an *improvement
notice* to bring the property up to a certain standard.

The council does not have to tell you how they found
out about your substandard property, so anyone – your
tenant, your nosy neighbour, your disgruntled ex – can
rat on you. It simply isn't worth the risk – *make sure
your property is in good condition before you rent it
out.*

Unfair though this may seem, you are not allowed to
recover the cost of upkeep and repairs by way of a
service charge; you are expected to finance them out of
the rent. So remember to charge enough rent to enable
you to do this. And see *A word on grants*, which
follows.

A word on grants

You might qualify for a grant to bring your property up
to standard. These grants are meant to help landlords to:

- make their properties fit for human habitation;
- upgrade habitable properties which need substantial repair;
- provide fire protection and escape (for self contained flats);
- improve heating and thermal insulation (eg lofts, tanks, cavity walls, double glazing);
- improve energy efficiency;
- improve fire safety (for all properties).

Before you become too excited, however, we should point out that grants usually have strings attached. The grant process is very involved and you will probably have to jump through a great many hoops before the authorities will part with any money. Moreover, you will not be allowed to start work until the grant has been approved, which might wreck your timetable.

There is, however, no harm in trying. You can start by calling your local council and asking to speak to someone from the private sector housing team.

Another, probably surer, source of help would probably be one of the energy saving schemes subsidised by central government in association with the various utilities. Many private landlords have had cavity wall insulation and loft lagging done for a fraction of the real cost. Provision seems to vary from area to area: ask around; and see also the *Power point* below.

The down side of tenants on Housing Benefit is discussed on pages 73–75. But one bonus of having a tenant on benefits is that you would be likely to qualify for FREE home improvements under HEES, the Government's Home Energy Efficiency Scheme. For example, a tenant over 60 years of age, and on benefits, might well qualify your property for a complete FREE central heating system with no strings attached except a promise not to raise the rent for a year after completion of the work.

Many landlords have had thousands of pounds' worth of free work done under this scheme. Telephone 0800 952 1555 for details (in some areas it is called the Eaga Partnership, but the concept is the same).

Are you insured?

Your insurance company will want to know what you are up to. Tell it in writing and keep a copy. You will find a sample letter on page 150 of this book and on the website. *Don't let your property until you have your insurer's go-ahead.*

If you do not tell your insurance company, it may be able to refuse to pay out on a claim, such as a fire caused by a tenant's negligence.

Many contents insurance policies have in their small print a get-out clause which means you will not be compensated for theft from your property unless entry has been forced. The insurance company may therefore be able to avoid paying out in the event of theft by your tenant (who of course has a key!).

A tenant in Felixstowe recently did a moonlight flit, taking the entire contents of the property with him. The landlord's insurers are, at the time of writing, refusing to pay out on his claim.

You will also need insurance against claims that may arise if your tenants are injured as a result of defects in your property or contents.

—We all hope that everything will go well for you, but in case it doesn't, you would be wise to have legal expenses cover. Many policies include legal expenses cover as a matter of course – check yours.

Make friends with the Small Landlords' Association (SLA), an organisation that is run by small landlords for small landlords. The SLA offers members their own insurance scheme. They say, 'For many members the savings compared to their previous insurer save their SLA subscription several times over'. Their scheme covers situations many insurers would reject out of hand, such as landlords who rent to asylum seekers. For details see *Useful Contacts* on page 160. You are not tied to the SLA for your insurance, however. There are bewildering numbers of insurance companies offering supposedly advantageous deals for landlords. Start with >http://www.quoted4mortgages.com<

Mortgaged property

Is your property mortgaged? If so, it will be a condition of your mortgage – unless, of course, you are buying it on a buy-to-let mortgage, in which case your lender will already have 'blessed' your plans – to obtain your bank/building society's consent to any letting. In practice it are unlikely to mind as long as the letting is on an assured shorthold tenancy (see below).

If you tell your mortgage lender, the good news is that it will 'bless' the arrangement. The bad news is that it will almost certainly charge you up to £100 for (alleged) administrative expenses. It may also decide to put up your interest rate. You may well have to pay up because it will just add it to the amount you already owe it. But before agreeing to pay extra interest, check to see that it really has the right to do this.

There is a school of thought that advises you to think carefully before involving your mortgage lender. Unlike your insurers, it may not really need to know, and your honesty may cost you dear (see above). This is something you must decide for yourself.

Letting leasehold property

Almost all flats and some houses are leasehold (see *Buzzwords*), which means that you own the lease but pay ground rent to the owner of the site on which the property stands. If your property is leasehold, you will almost certainly need the consent of your landlord (the person or organisation to whom you pay ground rent) to sublet. You should not be charged for this but the landlord can pass on any costs incurred, such as for having your tenancy agreement checked.

The normal arrangement is for you to continue to pay standing charges such as ground rent and buildings insurance. Set your rent at a level that covers these.

—If you are thinking of buying leasehold property to let, do make sure that there isn't an absolute ban on subletting!

A word on buy-to-let

What you are looking for is a good return on your money. Suppose property in your area is fetching low prices, while rents are fairly high. You look at a £50,000 house that can command £6,000 a year in rent, and you wonder if this offers a better return for your money than a building society. But – if this means that the property is expensive to maintain, and if it is unlikely to attract reliable tenants – you may find first that you get a poor return on your money, and second that the cost of borrowing makes the financial consequences even more severe for you. Remember that borrowing money for investment has a 'gearing' effect, so if things go well they go very well, and if the investment under-performs the damage is magnified.

Suppose you are looking to buy in what is already an expensive area: you may find that the rental income provides only a small percentage return on your money. However, you may benefit from good quality tenants and, perhaps, property price rises. There again, house prices can and do go down as well as up. Although you can see the bricks and mortar you are still speculating – and if you have a buy-to-let mortgage you are taking chances with borrowed money.

Or you might have a son or daughter going off to university or college in a town where lodgings are scarce and dear but house prices are fairly low. This consideration would normally rule out anywhere where property prices were high, such as Cambridge; but there may be bargains to be had in areas of low house prices but high rental demand. You may decide to buy a property near the campus and rent it to a group of students including your own offspring.

If you rent to students, make sure YOU are the ————— landlord! It can be difficult for a young person to 'police' a property, keep the rents coming in and stay friends with their fellow occupants.

With any luck, you reckon, you will be able to sell the house at a profit at the end of the three or four years. Many people have done this successfully. Bear in mind, however, that if the university town is a long way from where you live you may be unfamiliar with the area and could get stung.

'Yes,' we hear you say, 'That's fine; but I'd need a mortgage'. Until recently, people like you were in for a hard time. Most people go to building societies for their mortgages. Building societies exist primarily to enable people to buy their own homes, not to make a killing on the property market, and they are traditionally very unhappy about lending money on property to rent out. If a building society did offer a mortgage on such a property, it would set a higher rate of interest, demand large surcharges and very often refuse to take the rental income into account in assessing the borrower's ability to repay the loan.

New legislation, and an initiative by the Association of Rental Letting Agents (see *Useful Contacts* on page 159), changed that for ever. ARLA got together with several major lenders and launched the 'Buy-to-Let Scheme'. Borrowers can get loans without paying higher interest rates or surcharges and the lender will usually take the potential rental income into account in calculating the borrower's ability to repay the loan.

Do your homework

Buy-to-let is not a 'get rich quick' investment. You need to do your homework:

- how much would you have to pay for a suitable property?
- how much deposit would you have to pay up front?
- how much would you have to spend on doing it up?
- how much rent is it likely to command?

- what demand is there for rental property in that area?

- can you afford to pay the mortgage if the property is empty for any length of time?

- would the rent contribute sufficiently to the mortgage payments plus the maintenance, insurance, agent's fees and other outgoings?

Look for 'buy-to-let' on the web; you will be offered hundreds of sites, notably those of letting agents anxious to manage your property for you.

Try also to talk to several landlords who have tried buy-to-let. Then make up your own mind.

Here, meanwhile, is a whistle-stop tour of the pros and cons of borrowing money to buy a rental property.

Pros

- you may get – in theory at least – a better return on your money than you would in a savings account;

- the rent will contribute to the mortgage payments;

- you can keep an eye on your investment – no sharp young men in red braces can gamble with it;

- you can set the interest off against rent when calculating your profit for tax purposes;

- if property prices rise you are on to a good thing;

● there is a choice of fixed-rate or flexible mortgages to suit differing needs.

Cons

● few buy-to-let mortgage lenders will advance more than 80% of a property's value;

● you carry on paying off your mortgage even when the property is sitting empty;

● if you're getting on a bit you may have trouble borrowing the money over more than five or ten years;

● a good slice of your rental income may well go on paying a managing agent (many lenders insist you instruct one);

● property values can go down as well as up and you might find yourself owing more than your property is worth (the buzzword here is *negative equity,* and it is bad news);

● rents can go down as well as up;

● so can demand for rental property;

● you may – especially if your rental income is more than £15,000 a year – find yourself being charged tax on rent arrears, ie rents which have become payable but which you have not received. If you never get the rent, you can claim bad debt relief, but you are out of pocket in the meantime. See *A word on tax* on page 110.

Can you afford to keep up the payments even if you don't get any rent? The Small Landlords' Association (see page 160) reckons that as many as one letting in 20 results in disputes between landlord and tenant; and however easy getting shot of a bad tenant may seem in theory, there is always hassle involved. Little has changed since Shakespeare talked of 'the law's delay' and you could find yourself with a tenant who owes three months' rent and is clocking up arrears like a taxi meter while the local court seems unable to appreciate the urgency of your case. Meanwhile you are servicing a big loan on property that is not bringing you in a penny.

Finding a tenant

You can go it alone, or call in a letting agent, someone whose business it is to manage other people's property. Many High Street estate agents let property as well as selling it, but some agents specialise in letting only. See *Instructing a letting agent*, on page 57.

Going it alone is either free or fairly inexpensive and you get tax relief (see *A word on tax* on page 110) on the cost of any advertising. The down side is that you are on your own. Nobody is going to select your tenant, collect the rent for you, argue with a bad tenant or help you if things go wrong. If this worries you, consider using an agent.

—Inexperienced landlords often find it helpful to instruct an agent for their first let, then strike out on their own when they feel more confident.

Before you start searching

Forget the clichés – there are exceptions to every rule except one. *Be wary of letting property to friends or relations!* You of course will know the individuals better than we do; but ask yourself:

● can I put the transaction on a businesslike footing and keep it that way?

- can I be as firm with them as with a stranger, such as in insisting on regular rent payments and observance of rules?

- can I be sure of getting rid of them when the time comes?

Unless the answer to all three questions is a resounding YES, find a good excuse for turning them down without hurting their feelings.

Attracting a tenant

Before you start actively hunting for a tenant for yourself or instructing an agent to do so, you need to look carefully at the property you are offering. Many landlords forget that they are promoting a product – their property – and that good tenants are apt to be choosy.

Quite apart from being habitable, safe and in good repair, your property needs to be attractive. Here are some pointers:

- decorate in pale, neutral colours for maximum light and freshness;

- either have an agreement with your tenant ('You may put up pictures and posters provided you make good with filler and paint before you leave') or put up some old-fashioned picture rail from a DIY shop to enable your tenant to put up pictures without damaging your walls;

- good quality paint lasts longer than wallpaper and is easier and quicker to renew;

- durable, good quality carpets and curtains are essential, especially in an unfurnished property where they are not hidden by furniture. Cheap carpet is a bad buy. Your mantra here is *bombproof* – heavy domestic cords and Berber twists in neutral shades are very durable. Have them fitted by a reputable person and get a guarantee;

- kitchens need reliable appliances which are simple to operate (remember they are *your* responsibility if they go wrong);

- if you are letting furnished property, pay particular attention to the safety regulations for upholstered furniture (see page 39);

- offer plenty of storage space. Consider installing fitted wardrobes in bedrooms; and in furnished property beds with drawers underneath are a good idea;

- bathrooms and lavatories need to have extractor fans, good lighting and quality fittings, and tiles should be freshly grouted. Grubby grout is off-putting, and avocado baths are *passé*;

- a power shower is essential – and so is a non-slip surface to stand on.

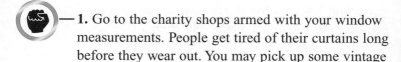**1.** Go to the charity shops armed with your window measurements. People get tired of their curtains long before they wear out. You may pick up some vintage

Sanderson or Colefax and Fowler for a few pounds, then spend on carpets the money you have saved on curtains.

2. The small ads are a rich source of nearly new bathroom fittings. £50 for a white bathroom suite with taps and waste is not unusual.

3. Revamping a kitchen need not cost a fortune. You can often spot complete two-year-old kitchens, discarded in their owners' frantic efforts to keep up with the Joneses, in the small ads for £100 or less. Add some new worktops (second-hand ones are rarely the right size) and you've saved yourself a four-figure sum.

Instructing a letting agent

Good agents will:

- find a suitable tenant, while leaving the final choice up to you;

- prepare and complete the letting agreement.

If your agents want to use their own letting agreement,—
check theirs against the one in this book to make sure it protects your interests.

The agents should also be able to:

- advise you on how much rent you should be charging;

- advise you about any refurbishment, repairs, etc, that should be done before letting (a little work now could mean an extra £100 a month later);

- hold any deposit in a separate account (ie *not* mixed up with the agents' own money) from which YOU get the interest;

- collect the rent and pass it on to you at once;

- keep proper records of money paid out and received;

- inspect the property regularly and let you know if anything needs attention;

- take all necessary steps to obtain vacant possession of the property when the letting ends;

- charge only a reasonable commission – that is, not more than 12.5–15% of rent paid plus VAT. Note that many agents charge the tenants too – if this bothers you, ask for details of their practices;

- have professional indemnity insurance so that you can be compensated if mistakes are made.

Having said this, we should mention that many agents offer several levels of service. Typically they are:

- Introduction only (sometimes called *let and vet*):
  - finding a tenant;
  - taking up references;

- ○ preparing the tenancy agreement (check to make sure it is the same as ours – see *Power point* above);
- ○ preparing the inventory and getting it signed;
- ○ collecting deposit and first month's rent.

After that you're on your own. Expect to pay a flat fee.

- Rent collection service:
  - ○ All of the above plus regular collection of rent. They might charge a flat fee, or a percentage of the rent.

- Full management:
  - ○ All of the above, plus all the day to day management: repairs, inspections, notices to quit, etc. This is the one you would probably want if you were going to be out of the country.

More homework

Before you decide on a particular agent, do your homework. Access the ARLA website (see *Power point* below) and download all the free literature you can conveniently digest (there is an awful lot of it). Then either use ARLA to find likely-looking agents in your area (see *Power point* below) or buy your local newspaper on the day that majors in property and note the details of all the letting agents.

Most agents will be happy to put you in touch with satisfied clients, but keep your eyes and ears open for other sources of information – word gets around. Meanwhile, here are the pros and cons of instructing an agent:

Advantages: An agent can do everything for you: this is helpful if, for example, you are letting your home while you are working abroad.

Disadvantages: This is going to cost money (although you can set the agent's fees against tax). How much depends on the individual agent. Also, you are handing over control to someone else – and there are plenty of incompetent agents around (see below).

–The rogue agent

Anybody can set themselves up as a letting agent without any qualifications or experience, and some do. Some are merely incompetent; but there are also rogue agents who collect rents and deposits from tenants and fail either to pass on the rents to the landlords or to return the deposits to the tenants. When a letting agent in Newmarket bankrupted herself without warning, the list of creditors (people to whom she owed money) was 12 pages long, and nobody ever found any of the money.

All those landlords lost large sums in rent, and were also legally responsible for returning the deposits to the tenants. This may seem unfair, especially as the landlords never saw the money in the first place, but it's the law. The rogue agent was prosecuted and found guilty. She did probation and the last time we heard of her she was working for a letting agent!

A good starting point in your search for a reliable agent is the Association of Residential Letting Agents (ARLA) – for details see *Useful Contacts* on page 159 – either by telephone or on their website >www.arla.co.uk< All ARLA agents must carry professional indemnity insurance and operate separate client bank accounts.

Going it alone

Let us suppose you decide on a DIY approach. The first step is:

Spreading the word

Ways of finding a tenant include:

- word of mouth (but beware of letting to friends or relations – see above);
- advertisements
  - in newspapers or magazines read by the kind of person you hope to attract (see *Power point* below)
  - in newspapers;
- cards in shop windows;

- notice boards in supermarket foyers.

—If you have a particular hobby or interest, you could consider advertising your property in a magazine aimed at that group of people. You might attract a fellow radio amateur/biker/euphonium player that way.

Many advertising papers are delivered free to all the homes in a particular area. Get hold of a few, ask how much they charge for a small ad, and try your luck.

If you go for the shop window or notice board approach, a typed notice is better than one that is handwritten. Remember it's your first contact with propsective tenants: make it legible and attractive. And omit your address (see below).

Other sources

Why not consider the following:

University or college

The accommodation officers may be willing to pass on a handout of your details.

Some universities or colleges inspect prospective rental properties before they put you on their list, others are simply glad of another address to hand out to students.

Make sure you know who is your tenant! If you find
yourself letting to the college housing office, this may
amount to a company let. This is not necessarily a bad
thing, but it won't be an assured shorthold tenancy as
we know it – for details see page 64.

Try, if you can, to liaise with the parents (who could,
for example, come up with the deposit and then put
pressure on the young people to behave!) rather than
their offspring. In any case, get all the students' names
on the tenancy agreement to make sure they are jointly
and severally (see *Buzzwords*) liable for the rent and for
any damage.

Hospitals

There never seems to be enough accommodation for
nurses and doctors and, as with universities and
colleges, there will probably be an official who will be
glad to add you to their database. The same
considerations apply as to universities and colleges (see
above).

Employers

Personnel (or human resources, or whatever they're
calling them this week) departments of big employers in
your area will usually be delighted to put you on their
database or display a card on their notice board. Many
will want short lets for employees who are new to the
area or on fixed-term contracts. Industries with highly
mobile workforces are a prime target.

— **A word on company lets**

By a company let, we mean one where your tenant is the company, not the individual. Many organisations like to have a pool of suitable rental property for their employees.

If you do let to a company, the tenancy agreement will not be an assured shorthold tenancy, which is for individuals only. In practice, the main difference between an assured shorthold tenancy and a company let will be that under the former sub-letting (ie by the tenant to a third party) is usually prohibited, whereas under the latter sub-letting must be allowed – but controlled so that the sub-tenant (the employee) does not get the statutory right to stay in your property indefinitely. The tenancy agreement in this book is not a company letting agreement, and you should take professional advice.

There are, however, advantages to company lets:

- a company might well be financially sounder than an individual (although it depends on the company – see below);

- rent may be paid in three or six month chunks in advance;

- companies often want long term lets for their staff and can offer you more continuity than some tenants can.

Possible snags are:

- the company might want to use its own rental agreement. If so, take legal advice if it differs significantly from ours;

- for the legal exemptions to apply you must be dealing with a company – not a private individual or a partnership;

- a foreign company (ie one not registered in the UK) could be a great nuisance if you need to claim for damage or unpaid rent.

Some companies are household names, but others may not be known to you. You can check them out instantly, by doing a search on the Companies House website: http://www.companieshouse.gov.uk

Planning your advertising

Advertisements in a local newspaper or magazine (national ones would probably cast your net too wide) can be expensive, but you do reach a larger readership than through shop windows, etc. Start by looking at other people's ads in the property section of your local newspaper and noting the accepted abbreviations that will save you money. Why pay for 'gas fired central heating' if you can get away with 'GFCH'?

Small ads usually give all or most of the following information:

- approximate location;

- any obvious selling points (eg 'quiet', 'newly dec', 'pte pkg', 'gdn' or 'nr shops');

- rent expected, adding 'exc' if your tenant will be responsible for utility bills and 'inc' if they will not;

- any special points (eg 'Refs reqd', 'Quiet N/S prof' or 'Sorry no pets');

- contact telephone number, box number (see *Power point* below) or possibly e-mail address.

Draft an advertisement that seems OK to you – remember that this is your first contact with your potential tenant, so waste a word or two saying how attractive your property is. Rosy started one ad for a smart modern studio with 'drop dead gorgeous' and received 37 replies.

Your checklist:

- be brief. This is a small ad, not an estate agent's blurb. That comes later (see *The blurb,* below);

- be honest. Don't say your property is immaculate if there are holes in the carpets and scuff marks on the walls. Prospective tenants will just blame you for wasting their time;

- be informative. Include all the relevant information. You are hoping to attract plenty of interest, but if you're advertising a town flat you don't want to waste time talking to people looking for a country cottage.

Then call the advertising department of your chosen publication and find out:

- the deadline – if the property section of your local newspaper comes out on a Friday, you may need to submit your ad by Wednesday noon. Don't miss the boat;

- the cost. Some tele-sales people are on commission and will try to sell you an elaborate package you don't need, such as a free insertion if you pay for three. One insertion in the right place, at the right time, will usually be enough.

You may be able to dictate the ad over the telephone, paying by credit card. If so:

- get them to send a copy of the invoice for your file – and keep it safe, because it's worth money to you in the form of tax relief;

- spell out anything potentially confusing;

- have the tele-sales girl or boy repeat the entire ad to you, especially the contact details. You can usually get a free insertion in the next issue if they goof seriously, such as getting your telephone number wrong, but their carelessness could lose you a week's rent.

—When advertising in a newspaper or magazine it is a good idea to use a box number if you are not in a tearing hurry. A box number costs a little extra but saves you fielding a lot of telephone calls at inconvenient times. We know of landlords who receive up to 50 enquiries from one ad; a box number allows some preliminary sifting before you start telephoning applicants.

Interlude

'She was poor but she was honest' – tenants on benefits

Sometimes you see something along the lines of 'Sorry no DSS' in property ads. This kind of discrimination has not been challenged in the courts – yet. For the moment you are free to pick and choose your tenants, and you may prefer not to let to anyone on benefits. Do not, however, close your mind to this possibility without considering the advantages and disadvantages.

Free improvements

A tenant on benefits may qualify you for some very valuable improvements to your property. See page 45 for details of the Government's free Home Energy Efficiency Scheme (HEES). The only string attached is that you must promise not to raise the rent for a reasonable time – usually one year – after the improvements have been completed.

Sources of supply

There are two likely sources of potential tenants on benefits:

- your local authority housing department;
- local homelessness charities and similar organisations.

Not all areas are well served by the latter. The national homelessness organisations such as Shelter tend to be better at giving legal advice than actually finding accommodation; but there are some wonderful local initiatives, often operating on a shoestring.

In the authors' own area a housing action group works hand in hand with the local authority and benefits agencies to match landlords with prospective lodgers and tenants.

Their relationship with landlords is exemplary. They will take careful note of the landlord's requirements and can often arrange a 'beauty parade' of prospective tenants, all armed with references. They will lend a hand with form filling for candidates on benefits and may even be able to provide deposits from their own funds or from related charities (that may be a good source of deposits). They can often advance the first month's rent too, which is a thing no local authority, however helpful, is likely to do (although see page 91 regarding the deposit guarantee scheme).

Potential tenants don't need to be on benefits to consult an action group; many people in good jobs who are new to the area approach the group rather than an agent, who may charge them extortionate fees for poor service.

To see what your local housing action group equivalent is, approach your local Citizen's Advice Bureau for details of organisations operating in your area.

Direct payment of rent

If you do take a tenant who qualifies for Housing Benefit, you can (with the tenant's agreement – you will be given a special form for you both to sign) arrange for the rent to be paid directly into your bank account. If a tenant on Housing Benefit gets behind with the rent, the housing authority can choose to pay you direct anyway, but as there usually have to be at least eight weeks' arrears before the arrangement kicks in, you may prefer to be paid direct from the beginning.

—Note, however, that you may not be able to command such a high rent as with a private tenant.

The Housing Benefit the authorities will pay out is based on:

● the tenant's age and entitlement (eg, a couple with one child would not be entitled to a four-bedroom house);

● what the local rent officer regards as the going rate for the accommodation you are offering – which may not be the same as what the private market will bear.

Setting a rent

The local authority is likely to ask a rent officer to inspect your property and set the level of rent. In theory you can expect an official with a clipboard to knock on your door. In practice the 'inspection' may simply be done in the office, based on a glance at the street map of your area and the rent officer's knowledge of the going rate for the kind of property you are offering.

Once this has been done, the local authority has set a rent and your tenant has moved in, you may face a longish wait for your money while your case works its way laboriously through the local authority system. You may be kept waiting for two months for the money while the paperwork moves slowly and majestically through the system. This is where the rent advance scheme offered by some homeless charities could come into its own. Ask about this.

If a tenant on benefits is unable to offer you a deposit,—
don't despair. Many local authorities run deposit
guarantee schemes (see page 91).

Coping with officialdom

This is not intended as a diatribe against local authorities, who for the most part do their best; but it is worth mentioning that officials can and do mislay documents and then deny ever having received them. This is often due to the 'If I can't find it on the computer system it doesn't exist' phenomenon. It can take many working days to transfer the information from a stack of forms onto the computer system and forms have been known to go AWOL before their details have been entered, and people can and do make typing errors in transferring information to their database. Of course, the inconvenience for you is the same whatever the reason for the hiccup. In your dealings with officialdom it pays to:

- open a file labelled with the address of your rental property;

- make a note of any reference number or code allocated to your case; write this in thick black felt tip on the file, and quote it in every communication – both by telephone and in writing – with the authority;

- keep a copy of everything you send or hand in;

- keep careful notes for your file of all telephone conversations, with dates and the name of the official you spoke to. You think you will remember, but in one month's time you will have forgotten all about it;

- get a signed receipt for everything you hand in and never, ever part with it until you have taken a copy;

- make friends with an official connected with your case, write their name and telephone extension

number on the front of the file in thick black felt tip
and call them regularly to ask about progress.

Clawing back overpayments

Having your tenant's Housing Benefit paid straight to
you can work very well. You get the money before your
tenant can spend it on riotous living or shoes for the
children. But beware! If, because of your tenant's
benefit fraud, the local authority pays out more money
than the tenant is entitled to – *even if you yourself are
totally unaware of anything untoward* – the local
authority will claw back the overpayment from *you*. You
have to sign a form agreeing to this, and every few
months your local authority will enclose a reminder
about it with your regular statement, so you cannot
plead ignorance.

They have the statutory power to recover this money
from you and, because they are generously rewarded by
central government for doing so, they will do their
utmost to exercise that power.

They will do it either by:

● demanding payment from YOU then and there; or
● deducting the overpayment in instalments from the
  ongoing rent.

Either way is bad news. If you don't pay, local
authorities have the power to take you to court for the
money, and recent case law indicates that they will win.
A County Court judgment (see below) against you

would affect your future credit rating. It sure as hell ain't fair on an innocent landlord, but that is what will happen.

You are then supposed to claim the money back from your tenant, but this is stressful at best and costly at worst. Suppose you buy our *Recovering a debt* book in this series and use it to get a County Court judgment against your tenant. This is quite straightforward; but you may never see your money. You can't get blood out of a stone. The judge will take the tenant's income into account and may order them to pay off their debt in such small instalments that you might as well have written off the money in the first place. This is, of course, a worst-case scenario, and if you choose your tenant carefully it may never happen to you.

The poverty trap

Many landlords have problems with tenants who, after a time on benefits, find work and receive a pay cheque instead of a benefit giro. You would think this was good news for everyone, and of course in many ways it is, but many tenants have trouble paying their rent and Council Tax out of their wages.

We shan't go into detail here, but being in work usually means losing entitlement to Housing Benefit and Council Tax Benefit, not to mention the free school meals, free prescriptions and other goodies that people on benefits receive. There are schemes to cushion the blow – the tenant can usually get some extra Housing

Benefit to tide them over until the first pay cheque –
but we know of several good tenants who have had to
leave their rented property because they could no longer
afford to live there.

That's enough of that: back to the process of choosing
your tenant.

Fielding phone calls

Be on your guard —————————————————

Your prospective tenants are complete strangers. Most
people are harmless, but statistically you may well meet
some doubtful characters eventually. To protect
yourself, consider some or all of the following when
fielding phone calls (or indeed opt for a box number –
see *Power point*, on page 68 above):

● be aware that not all callers may be looking for
accommodation, and that some villains can be very
plausible;

● don't give your full address in any advertisement – a
contact telephone number is enough;

● when someone rings to enquire about your property;
write down whatever telephone number they give
you, then ring 1471 afterwards to check that the two
numbers are the same;

● avoid giving any personal information – such as the
fact that you live alone – in your advertisement or
on the telephone;

- don't answer late-night telephone calls. People can call again at a reasonable hour, or forget the whole thing;

- if the call turns obscene or malicious, resist the temptation to burst into tears (they'll love it) or make wisecracks (they'll call you again to see if you can keep it up). Just put down the receiver, do a swift 1471 in case they've been careless, and if you feel it is justified, tell both your telephone company and the police;

- don't give a candidate the address of the property until you are sure you want to meet them;

- before meeting a candidate, always call them at home or at work, ostensibly to double-check the time of your appointment;

- listen to your inner voice. If you don't like the sound of them, don't meet them face to face.

'Telephone vetting'

Be near the telephone, armed with pen and paper, as soon as your ad appears – and that can mean as early as 7 a.m. In many localities, an attractively worded 'to let' advertisement brings in at least 20 enquiries. These are like popcorn; there are a few calls early on, then a fusillade of enquiries, tapering off to a few stragglers a day or so later.

Unless you are using a box number (see Power point, on page 68 above), make sure you are at home on the day your ad appears. Many people are nervous of answering

machines and ring off without leaving a message, and
you could lose the ideal tenant that way.

The first telephone contact gives you an opportunity of
checking your prospective tenants unobtrusively. Do
remember, however, that your potential tenants will be
checking you out too!

You are looking for someone who will:

● pay the rent;

● take care of your property;

● be a considerate neighbour.

This person is going to live in your property and you
have every right to turn down anyone you find
uncongenial or who you think might cause annoyance
to you or your neighbours (but see *Beware of
discrimination*, below).

Three questions you are certain to be asked

● do you accept children?

● do you accept pets?

● are people on benefits welcome? (for the pros and
cons of this one, see *She was poor but she was
honest* on page 68).

You can, of course, decide what line you are going to
take, and stick to it. If you cherish your soft

furnishings, or if the property itself is not very child-friendly, say so.

If you loathe dogs and cats and hate the thought of hairs and worse on your carpets, say firmly 'Sorry, no pets' and hang on until someone comes along who shares your views.

If you hate the idea of someone on Income Support or Jobseeker's Allowance, or whatever they're calling it this week, occupying your property, stick to your guns. It isn't against the law, yet.

Another way of handling these questions is to keep your options open. Say cautiously, 'It depends on the individual children/pets/people'; see the people, children and pets for yourself and use your common sense.

Be meticulous

Sift candidates as you talk on the telephone, making notes to keep on file.

Use a fresh sheet of paper for each caller. It is surprisingly easy to mislay people's details unless you are organised. That is why the checklist below will be helpful.

You may find yourself rejecting several hopefuls before you actually make an appointment to show anyone around. This is to be expected.

Checklist: first telephone contact with prospective tenant

Consider printing out several of these.

Candidate's name............................

Where do they come from?..................................

Contact telephone number............................

At work [ ] student [ ] on benefits [ ]

Can they give references? [ ]

Deposit available? [ ]

Any other information they offer about themselves

Arrange to show around [ ]

Date..

Time......................................

Put on backup list [ ]

Not suitable [ ]

Another interlude: the blurb

This is a typed description of your property. Send or fax
to prospective tenants who have survived the first sift.
Include such information as:

- your name and a contact telephone number;
- the exact address of the property;
- directions for getting there if this is likely to be a
  problem;
- distances from shops, public transport;
- anything else you think is likely to be useful.

For example, prospective tenants of a family house will
want to know about schools, while an elderly person
will want to know how far away are the shops.

- a brief description of the accommodation;
- how much Council Tax is payable (see below);
- what utilities are available and who pays for them
  (eg is the water supply metered? Is the gas/electric
  on a card meter?);
- the monthly rent;
- the deposit.

The blurb gives short-listed candidates the necessary
information in a handy, user-friendly form and saves
you answering a great many questions many times over.

It also makes sure they don't mislay your contact details.

Once you have drafted it, keep your blurb on file or, even better, on disk, for future use. Remember you may need to update it from time to time

Face to face

You will probably have to set half a day or so aside for showing people around and interviewing them.

Remember – you don't know these people. All you know about them is what they have told you themselves. If you are haunted by the fate of estate agent Suzy Lamplugh, who left the office to show a client around a property and was never seen again, nobody can blame you for being cautious.

If you have not done much interviewing or showing-around before, consider having a dry run with a friend playing the part of a prospective tenant.

Try to arrange for a friend or, if you have one, your dog to be with you when you do meet candidates. Your friend can check 'em out as well and help you by taking notes; and if your normally benign hound growls and goes all stiff-legged, ask yourself why.

Allow plenty of time for each prospective tenant. Half an hour is about right. It should give you enough time to show the prospective tenant around and interview them as you go, plus a few minutes to make notes after they've left.

Be prepared for the occasional 'no show'. A spare half an hour is no bad thing; you can use the time to bring your notes on the other candidates up to date.

—Always take notes. As any experienced interviewer will tell you, interviewees seem to merge into each other after the first half dozen or so.

Remember, yours will not be the only property on the candidates' list. People can and do drop out. Don't stop noting names and telephone numbers and don't stop interviewing over the telephone, even if you think you have the perfect tenant plus a couple of spares.

Keep a record of suitable tenants who didn't quite make it first time. Then, next time you have a property vacant, you can call them and maybe save yourself the cost of a newspaper advert and a lot of interviewing.

When each candidate arrives ...

Have their first contact details in front of you (see page 79) and a list of points to mention (Council Tax? television licence?).

Give them your blurb if you have not already sent it (see page 80, above).

Try to envisage the kinds of questions you are likely to be asked (see *Three questions you are certain to be asked*, on page 77 above), and have your answers ready.

Here are some points to consider:

1. Are you prepared to accept a tenant on benefits?

See *She was poor but she was honest* on page 68.

2. If not, are you satisfied that your prospective tenant will be able to pay the rent?

We're not talking about demanding a complete statement of means here, just some indication that there is enough money coming in from a reliable source.

3. Has your prospective tenant got either the deposit or the means to obtain it (there are schemes to help Housing Benefit clients with deposits – see page 91)?

4. Does the prospective tenant seem to be clean, tidy and punctual?

We would reject out of hand anyone who turned up late for their interview without a good reason, wearing anything other than clean clothes and 'shining morning face'. This is of course a matter of personal preference and you are welcome to disagree.

5. Is your prospective tenant being frank with you?

Beware of anyone who seems unwilling to talk about their employer, their previous landlord, etc. You will of course, in any case, ask for references – and follow them up (see *References* on page 87).

6. Remember that the rent, which you have set after carefully researching the going rates for your area, is not negotiable. If a prospective tenant wants to haggle, turn them down flat.

7. Make clear your views on things such as smoking, pets, etc, and stick to your guns.

8. Is there anything about the prospective tenant which might annoy you or your neighbours? Someone intent on keeping several dogs or learning the saxophone might not be popular.

9. Be businesslike, but listen to your own gut reactions too. If there seems something faintly suspect about a prospective tenant, something you can't quite put your finger on, there is probably a good reason. Trust your intuition. You will not often be wrong.

Be patient. Shyness and nervousness are no indication of a bad tenant.

They're checking you out too ...

Remember that while you are cautiously assessing your prospective tenant, *you* are being checked out too. Be punctual and have the property looking as attractive and welcoming as possible.

Some candidates may have several places to view. Make sure you hand out copies of your blurb (see page 80 above) to remind them what you are offering.

Accepting and rejecting

Never decide on the spot, however strong your gut feeling about someone. Say 'I'll let you know', name a day or time to call them, and keep your promise. Then use the time to follow up references.

Beware of discrimination —————————

Race discrimination is against the law. Even if you draft a racially discriminatory ad, no responsible newspaper will publish it.

You must not turn away a prospective tenant on grounds of race or colour. Apart from the fact that you might be turning down the perfect tenant, you could be committing a criminal offence.

Sex discrimination is also unlawful (but see exceptions below).

Discrimination on grounds of sexual orientation is not unlawful – yet, but only because the UK has so far failed to implement Article 13 of the Treaty of Amsterdam.

Legal lore

Sex discrimination is allowed in the provision of hostel-style accommodation, where for reasons of decency and propriety 'mixed bathing' is prohibited. Similarly, if you are letting a room in your own home you can also choose the sex of your lodger.

'No DSS' is not (yet) unlawful, although it may by implication discriminate against people from ethnic minorities and, for example, single mothers.

The Disability Discrimination Act 1995 makes it unlawful to discriminate against a disabled person because of their disability. Disability in this context includes mental as well as physical impairment. The Act applies specifically to residential property – so as landlord you cannot turn someone down because of disability, or offer them less favourable terms (eg, higher rent) than other candidates. Moreover, if the disabled person sues you the burden of proof is on you to show that you did not treat the disabled person less favourably because of their disability. (You can, of course, still reject a disabled candidate for some other, unrelated reason – such as bad references or inability to look after the property in accordance with the terms of the rental agreement.)

You are not under an obligation to let to a disabled person accommodation that presents them with a health and safety risk. Nor do you have to let to someone without the mental capacity to enter into a binding contract. The Act does not apply to small owner-occupied premises – which basically exempts people taking in lodgers.

Be nice

In turning anybody down, be kind and tactful. Nobody likes to feel rejected. Emphasise how difficult it was to make your choice. Word gets around. The unsuccessful candidates will inevitably talk to their friends and colleagues, and you would prefer them to speak well of you.

When you call your chosen tenant to inform them of their good fortune, *you must tell them that the deal is subject to satisfactory references* – see below.

Never worry about possible loss of income if you are slow in establishing your tenant. It is better to have a lean couple of weeks while you seek out the perfect tenant than to install one in haste and regret it at leisure.

References

Once you have made your choice, it is time to do some serious checking. However charming your prospective tenant seems, the two key questions are always:

- can your tenant pay the rent?
- will your tenant look after your property?

Nothing can guarantee a 'Yes' to both questions, but you can reduce the risks by:

- asking for references;
- following them up;
- taking a deposit (see below).

Do not rely on references that the tenant hands you. A colleague once interviewed a prospective tenant whose glowing testimonial, supposedly from the tenant's employer, turned out to be bogus. Well, to be precise, the headed paper was genuine, the tenant was who he said he was, but when our colleague telephoned the firm she found that the man had been sacked for dishonesty. If our colleague had been lax about checking him out, she could have let her property to a cheat.

Always look for:

- a financial reference, such as from an employer (is your tenant's job secure?);
- a reference from a previous landlord (why did he/she leave?);

- a personal reference from a responsible person who has known the prospective tenant for at least three years.

Take up the references. A sample reference request is on page 152.

Some referees will be more forthcoming over the telephone than in a letter: listen carefully and note any hesitation or too-careful choice of words. Nobody likes to speak ill of anyone, but there are ways of leaving things unsaid.

Serious checking

We know another landlord who was defrauded by a tenant with immaculate references from both his employer and his bank. If the landlord had checked more thoroughly he would have thought twice about granting him a tenancy. This man had recently arrived in the area and opened a new bank account; but he had County Court judgments against him in another part of the country; and his creditworthiness was nil.

Much financial information about people is confidential, and is jealously guarded by the Data Protection Act 1998. There are, however, sources of information that are publicly accessible:

- the Register of County Court Judgments – see *Useful Contacts* on page 164 – this costs £4;

—BUT this register does not include High Court judgments (which do not figure on any register), so really big debts can go unrecorded.

● the Individual Insolvency Register – see *Useful Contacts* on page 164 – keeps details of bankruptcy and individual voluntary arrangements (a sort of half way house between solvency and insolvency) and does not make a charge.

Additionally, some agents seek information from a licensed credit reference agency, most of which use 'credit scoring systems' and then allocate a pass mark to predict whether or not people are a good credit risk. See *Yellow Pages* for your local agencies, or call *Talking Pages* on 0800 600 900 for a free nationwide trawl.

—Using a credit reference agency will of course cost you and may not be totally reliable. In a spirit of research we paid good money for an agency to check out someone who to our certain knowledge had judgments against him, and he came out squeaky clean.

Deposits

Many landlords ask prospective tenants for a substantial deposit in addition to the first month's rent. One or two months' rent would be normal – do not ask for more than two months rent. This sum can be used to cover any unpaid rent, pay the cost of cleaning the property when the tenant leaves and make good any damage the tenant has done. The deposit (or what is left after such deductions) should be returned to the tenant at the end of the letting period. This lets you take the deposit if the tenant breaks the rules and thus causes you loss.

Deposits for tenants on benefits

You may think that deposits would be out of the question for tenants on benefits (see *She was poor but she was honest* on page 68); but you would be wrong.

Many local authorities run a deposit guarantee scheme for lodgers and tenants on benefits. Typically, the local authority gives the landlord a guarantee or bond (not actual money – see below) to cover a maximum of one month's rent. The bond is handed to the landlord as a deposit. In return for this, the lodger pays a small sum – typically £5 or £10 – to the local authority and promises:

- to pay the rent promptly;
- not to cause any damage;
- to pay the council for any damage that is caused.

If there is any damage at the end of the tenant's stay, the local authority – not the tenant – pays the landlord. The local authority then tries to recover the cost from the tenant; but meanwhile you will have had your money.

Additionally, some housing charities can arrange deposits either from their own funds or from other charities. Your local Citizen's Advice Bureau will have lists of charities operating in your area.

Ex-service charities such as SSAFA (Forces Help) can
sometimes provide deposits for old comrades who have
fallen on hard times. They may treat the deposit as a
gift to the individual, not a loan, which means that if
you have to use the deposit SSAFA will not ask you for
their money back.

*Remember that a deposit is the tenant's money, not
yours.* You might have recourse to it in future; but for
the moment you can't touch it. Recognised letting
agents keep deposit money separated from their own
money, and so should you.

It is wise, therefore, to put your tenant's deposit in an
interest-bearing account that is separate from your own
finances. Who gets the interest on the money is a matter
to be agreed between you and your tenant.

We know a few saintly landlords who pick accounts that
pay high interest and pass onto their departing tenants
the interest their deposits have earned, but this is of
course optional. Intelligent Finance, for example,
currently operates a high interest account that enables
you to keep money in several different 'pots' with
names chosen by you. You might consider opening one
of these with your tenant's first name and keeping the
monthly statement in your file.

The nitty gritty

You and the tenant need to agree on the following.

- *The extent of the property included in the letting.*
  This may seem blindingly obvious, but will the
  letting include the garage, the cellar, the locked shed
  where you store your valuable tools, etc?
  - *What contents are included in the letting.* See our
    advice on inventories on page 139.

- *Who the tenant(s) will be.* You should include in the
  letting agreement as joint and several (see
  Buzzwords) tenants all the *adults* who will occupy
  the property. This may, for example, include
  husband, wife, elderly parent, grown-up son and
  son's live-in girlfriend. Your tenants' visitors do not
  count. Nor do children under 18.

- *The length of the initial period* (see *Buzzwords*). As
  you cannot get the property back for six months
  unless the tenant breaks their agreement, we suggest
  there should be an initial fixed period and that this
  should be not less than six months.

- *The amount of rent, and the date it is due each
  month.* The sample tenancy agreement (see
  page 120) requires the tenant to pay the rent
  monthly. If you want the rent paid by standing order,
  your tenant should complete a standing order form
  (ask your bank to supply one).

- *The amount of deposit.* The deposit will be refundable, unless your tenant fails to keep their side of the agreement.

- *Who is liable for Council Tax, water charges, television licence, gas, oil, electricity and telephone.* Our sample agreement stipulates that the tenant will pay all of these. If you want to make other arrangements, you need to add the following words to Clause E of the tenancy agreement:

  'The Landlord is to pay [Council Tax/water charges for the property] [charges for oil/gas/electricity supplied to the property]'.

- *Whether or not children or pets may live at the property.* Our agreement as it stands does not allow either unless you agree. As we said before, you can always look at the individual case and judge for yourself: one child but not seven; a cat but not a pack of hounds.

- *Who is responsible for repairs, redecoration, etc.* Our tenancy agreement obliges the tenant to keep the property clean, tidy and in good decorative order and to keep equipment and appliances in good repair. The tenant is not expected to improve your property or its contents. You remain responsible for structural repairs – except for any made necessary by the tenant's damage to your property.

- *What state the property must be in when it is handed back.* The tenant must hand everything back in the same condition as when the letting began. If extra work is required to restore everything to its original condition, our tenancy agreement provides for professional cleaning of carpets, curtains, etc to be paid for from the tenant's deposit.

- *The inventory.* You will find this on page 139 and on the website and you should 'top and tail' it to suit.

Filling in the tenancy agreement

You have chosen your tenant and taken up references. It is now time to go through the legal formalities. Read these instructions carefully, then follow them meticulously, step by step. Do not cut corners.

Now print off the following from the website:

- Tenancy Agreement (Original) – marked *Original* in top right hand corner;

- Tenancy Agreement (Duplicate) – marked *Duplicate* in top right hand corner.

- *You cannot afford to be slapdash about this. To* 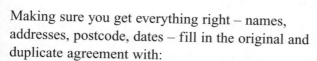 *protect your legal rights you MUST follow the instructions below. Refer to the worked example for guidance.*

Making sure you get everything right – names, addresses, postcode, dates – fill in the original and duplicate agreement with:

- *name and address of landlord(s)* including all co-owners;

95

- *name and address of tenant(s)* – include all adults who will occupy the property;
- *property address;*
- *initial period* (we suggest not less than six months);
- *amount of rent;*
- *date* on which rent is due each month;
- *deposit;*
- *variations (if any) of standard letting provision* (if none, state 'none');
- *inventory* (two copies) – you then attach one to the original agreement and the other to the duplicate.

When you have dealt with all the issues above, you can now deal with the tenancy agreement as follows:

You:

- sign and date the original agreement only;
- sign the inventory.

The tenant(s):

- sign and date the duplicate agreement only;
- sign the inventory.

(If you are dealing with more than one tenant, all tenants must sign the duplicate agreement and inventory.)

Now *you*:

- give the tenant(s) the original agreement, signed by you;

- take from the tenant(s) the duplicate agreement, signed by them;

- collect the deposit and give a receipt (you will find a sample in this book and on the website);

- collect the first instalment of the rent and give a receipt (you will find a sample in this book and on the website);

- hand over the key.

We know a new landlord who had a dry run of this procedure with a friend, to be sure of getting it right when it came to the real thing.

On page 133 we have explained the Standard Letting Provisions principally for your benefit. Consider giving your tenant(s) a copy of the explanation to keep.

Congratulations! You have a legally binding tenancy agreement.

Don't leave it up to your tenant to keep officials and utilities informed. They might forget. See the checklist below.

- tell the Council Tax department about the new tenant;

- read the electricity meter, call the electricity supplier

and ask for a bill. At the same time give them the name of the new tenant and date of moving in;

● do the same with the gas and water suppliers.

Before the tenant moves in

Here is your checklist of things to do before the tenant moves in.

● make or update inventory;
● take electricity meter reading, ask for a bill to today's date and inform supplier of name of new occupant;
● take gas meter reading, ask for bill to today's date and inform supplier of name of new occupant;
● take water meter reading (if applicable). In any case, inform water supplier of name of new occupant;
● call the Council Tax department and inform them of name of new occupant.

Now arrange to visit the property with your tenant and:
● show where cleaning materials, spare light bulbs, hoover, etc, are;
● go over procedure for emergencies;
● show electricity turn-off point;
● show gas turn-off point;
● show water turn-off point;
● show how to operate and maintain fire safety equipment (eg smoke alarms);

- show how to operate gas or electric fires;

- show how to operate appliances (washer, cooker, fridge, microwave, water softener, power shower, whatever) and show where to find instruction books;

- show how to operate central heating and hand over instruction book;

- show how to operate window safety catches, etc;

- go over procedure for security, intruder alarms, etc, and hand over any instruction books;

- go over arrangements for your inspection visits;

- hand over keys and say where a spare key may be found in an emergency (eg with a trusted neighbour);

- hand over tenant's checklist (see below);

- hand over record book (see *Power point* below);

- hand over a welcome pack (suggested contents: fresh milk, sugar, tea, coffee, a loaf of bread, butter and maybe a bottle of wine, a bunch of flowers or a lettuce from your garden) – whatever it takes to make them feel wanted.

Tenant's guide

Few tenants will take in all the information you throw at them during your welcome visit. It is sensible, therefore, to provide them with a list to stick inside a cupboard door or on a corkboard for easy reference. You might include:

- your contact details;
- where to find the turn-off points for gas, electricity and water;
- contact numbers for utilities and council;
- other contact numbers where appropriate, eg plumber, CORGI installer, etc., in case you are on holiday when disaster strikes;
- a list of instruction manuals, etc provided;
- a reminder of what repairs, etc, for which they are responsible (we suggest you hand over a set of working appliances and then make the tenant responsible for keeping them working);
- name and contact details of keyholder;
- a reminder of the date rent is due.

During the tenancy

And so you have installed the tenant in your property.

Collecting the rent

- A good tenant will pay the rent without being nagged. However, if you need to demand payment, you MUST do so in writing and put your name and address on your demand, otherwise it will not be valid. See the sample rent demand on page 153.

- If your tenants pay their rent weekly (or if your tenancy agreement refers to a weekly amount) you are required by law to provide your tenant with a rent book. Buy a proper one from a stationer's. An old exercise book won't do.

- It is of course sensible to keep an up-to-date account of rent payments, however the rent is paid. See *Record keeping*, below.

Record keeping

Even if *you* are inclined to be relaxed about record keeping, the Inland Revenue will expect you to keep all your records for at least six years, so you had better start as you mean to go on – and that means being organised.

- Print off several receipts for rent (use the sample on page 154 and the blank on the website). Give receipts and keep copies, even if the rent is paid direct into your bank account.

- Buy yourself a sturdy file. Write on it the address of the property and the tenant's name in thick black felt tip pen. You will need to open a new file for each new tenant.

Inside the front cover write:

- contact details for your tenant;
- the date the tenancy started;
- the amount of deposit paid;
- the amount of rent.

In the file you will keep:

- the tenancy agreement signed by your tenant;
- the inventory signed by your tenant;
- your tenant's references;
- copies of all correspondence;
- copies of all relevant documents (eg gas safety certificate);
- details of any expenditure (eg invoices – vital if you are to claim it against tax).

As time goes by you will build up quite a dossier. You may like to use the list on page 157 to record useful details: reference numbers for the council and the various utilities, details of any repairs, etc – all with the minimum of effort.

We know an experienced landlord with several properties who issues each new tenant with an A5 hardback notebook. On the flyleaf of this 'log book' insert:

- tenant's name;
- date of arrival;

- date rent is payable each month;
- amount of rent and deposit paid;
- any notes (eg 'water included').

On the left of each double page spread the tenant writes down anything that needs attention, while the right hand side does double duty as a record of rent paid and action taken to rectify any defects. That way both landlord and tenant have an ongoing record.

Increasing the rent

- You can *agree* a rent increase with your tenant at any time.
- You can't *impose* a rent increase during the initial period, or the first year, whichever is longer. After that unless the tenant agrees your proposed increase
  - you must use a special form, Form 5.
  - you must give the tenant one month's notice of the increase. The tenant may appeal to the Rent Assessment Committee.
- You must leave twelve months between increases.

Other changes to the tenancy

- You can *agree* changes to the tenancy at any time.

- You can't *impose* changes during the initial period. After that unless the tenant agrees your proposed change you must use a special form, Form 1.

If things go sour

It needs goodwill on both sides to make a letting work. If you are faced with an irreconcilable dispute, the most straightforward solution is for you to exercise your right to repossess the property.

Try within reason to avoid court proceedings, which can be lengthy, stressful and expensive.

Getting 'em out – repossession

Most tenants pay their rent in full and on time and leave on the appointed date. The next section deals with the others.

Unless your tenants have seriously and persistently let you down (the most obvious way being failing to pay the rent), you cannot repossess your property until the end of the initial period. But you can't step straight back into the property just because the initial period has ended – you must serve a statutory notice, the 'Landlord's Notice of Intention to Apply for Possession'.

Legal lore

Although this is a statutory notice (ie the period of notice and the information the document contains are laid down by law), the law does not prescribe the precise wording.

Now here is a step-by-step guide to repossessing your property by notice, which you may choose to follow whether or not your tenants have kept their side of the bargain.

You will find a worked example of the notice on page 156.

Take two copies of the notice and fill in:

- *name and address of tenant.*

  If there is more than one tenant, include the names of all adult tenants. Their address will usually be the address of the rental property, unless they have moved out.
- *your name and address;*
- *address of the rental property;*
- *possession date.*

If you are serving the notice within a fixed period of the tenancy (whether the initial fixed period or a further fixed period), the possession date must not be earlier than two months from the date the tenant receives your notice. For safety's sake, allow an extra week: a total of two months, one week.

Example: The fixed period is 1 January to 30 June. So, to get them out immediately the fixed period comes to an end, you need to serve the notice no later than 30 April – but for safety's sake do so by 23 April.

If you are serving the notice after any fixed period has ended, the possession date must be the day before the rent is next due, plus two months, although if the rent is next due within seven days we suggest you add another month for safety's sake.

Example: The fixed period has expired. The tenancy continues. The tenant pays the rent on the first day of each month. The day before that is the last day of the previous month. Add two months. So if you serve notice on 10 June, the earliest possession date will be 31 August.

● *date*;
● *your signature.*

You can now serve the notice on the tenants. There are two ways of doing this:

● in person (this may not be practicable: for example, if you are living a long distance away. It may also require bottle);
● by first class post, recorded delivery.

Legal lore

Lawyers *serve* documents that other people send, deliver or hand over. It comes to the same thing. Don't let it worry you.

In person

Give the tenant – or all of them if you have more than one – both copies of the notice and get them to sign one copy and return it to you. They keep the other copy.

By post

Send both copies by recorded delivery, and in a covering letter ask the tenants to sign and return one copy. Provide a stamped addressed envelope for this. The clerk in the Post Office will give you a stamped recorded delivery slip. Keep the slip as proof of posting.

When the tenants leave

This section applies equally to all tenants, good and bad:

Before moving day

- arrange to inspect the property;
- check the contents against the inventory.

On moving day

- return the deposit to the tenants, less any deductions for:
  - unpaid rent;
  - damage;
  - missing items;
  - cleaning costs.

—If you do deduct anything from the deposit, give the tenant a written calculation showing how you arrived at your figures.

Make sure you get a forwarding address.

—**If the tenants refuse to budge**

Or if they fail in any other way to keep their part of the bargain, you may need to apply to a court for an order compelling them to leave.

—Remember, it is a criminal offence to harass your tenants, or to remove them without a court order. Even when you have a court order, you can't take matters into your own hands. If the tenants won't comply with your court order, you must instruct the court bailiffs to evict the tenants for you.

You could face a massive compensation claim and unwelcome exposure in the tabloid press if you take the law into your own hands.

There is at the time of writing a 'quickie' procedure (whose Sunday name is the 'accelerated possession procedure under County Court Rules [CCR] Order 49') for the swift repossession of property let on an AST. No court hearing is necessary. However, there are two snags with the quickie procedure:

- An application under the quickie procedure cannot include a claim for rent arrears. This gives you a choice. You can use the quickie procedure for speed and – if you really think the tenant is able to pay you – start separate debt recovery proceedings for the unpaid rent. Alternatively, you can seek possession and the arrears in one action, but there will be a court hearing.

- The Human Rights Act 1998 confers on tenants the right to a hearing where they plead 'exceptional hardship'. In such circumstances there must be a court hearing, despite the intention of the quickie procedure to avoid this.

If you wish to use the quickie procedure, ask your local County Court for Form N5B. Otherwise (if, for example, you want to combine your repossession with a claim for rent arrears), you need to start with a prescribed Section 8 form. Court proceedings are, however, outside the scope of this book. You may need professional legal help.

A word on tax

Well, a few pages, actually.

—Unless you are very streetwise indeed, it may be worth handing your tax affairs over to a professional, whose expertise could well save you their fees (on which you can in any case claim tax relief).

—Before we start, we must make clear that we do not know you, *we do not know your individual circumstances and we can give you only the most general advice, based on tax law at the time of writing.*

Tax rules are constantly changing and evolving, and you cannot rely on a book which is even a year old to reflect the latest developments. Apart from financial journalists (for a broad view try the Money sections of the quality newspapers), consult the real tax gurus:

- the Inland Revenue: Go to >www.inlandrevenue.gov.uk< for general information. You can download IR literature; two key booklets are IR87, for one-property landlords, and IR150 for landlords with several rental properties;

- at your local Inland Revenue office for individual help;

- the professional advisers, such as your accountant.

Income tax

All income from property rentals in the UK is subject to tax. The Inland Revenue tends to treat it as investment income – that is, on a par with stocks and shares. Any landlord who has worked their fingers to the bone decorating a property and preparing it for its new occupants would take issue with that, but rules is rules.

The good news is that only your *profit* from renting is taxable. You are allowed to deduct your expenses – even the cost of this book (see below).

If you let *furnished* property, you will normally be allowed a standard 10% for wear and tear on furnishings and appliances in addition to one-off expenses such as plumbing or electrical repair bills. If you claim this, you do not have to give the Inland Revenue an itemised account of how you spent the money, and if you spend less than 10% of your rental income (chance would indeed be a fine thing!) you can still claim this allowance.

Whether or not you as an individual will have to pay tax on your letting income will depend on how much profit you make after expenses, and how much taxable income you have already.

When filling in your tax return, the law requires you to declare

- last year's rental income receivable, calculated from 6 April to 5 April in the following year;

- your expenses – what the property has cost you over the same period.

You will then pay tax on your net rental income – that is, the annual rent less 'allowable' expenses.

You will save a lot of time and effort in working out your net rental income if you:

- keep good records (see *Record keeping* on page 101) of
  ○ rent received;
  ○ expenses paid.

Open a separate bank account for your rental income and outgoings, so that you will receive bank statements whose day to day record of transactions will back up your own figures.

Your receipted invoices may be worth money to you in tax relief. Keep them safe!

Be fair. Be honest. Be reasonable.

Here are some of the things you may be able to claim against tax:

- agent's fees;
- Council Tax (if you are responsible for this – and in any case for any Council Tax you have had to pay between tenants);
- insurance premiums (buildings and contents);
- repairs and maintenance (other than the 10% allowance for wear and tear, so you could claim a plumber's bill but not new curtains);
- utility service bills (if you are responsible for them – and in any case for any utility bills you have had to pay between tenants);
- gas and electricity safety checks and certificates;
- interest on loans to buy/improve your rental property (but not the credit card debts you've just run up to pay for your holiday in Corfu);
- lease renewal expenses;
- removal expenses (eg to transport contents to rental property);
- subscription to SLA;
- advertising;
- extra fees to mortgage lender, etc;
- any legal, accountancy or other professional fees you have had to pay;
- the cost of this book;

- relevant telephone calls and postage;
- relevant stationery – which could include your printer cartridges;
- your mileage for visiting the property to inspect it and/or collect the rent.

Here are some expenses you *can't* normally claim:

- personal expenses, such as your own time;
- capital costs, for example buying the property (though you may be able to set them off against Capital Gains Tax if you sell the property later);
- upgrading costs (but interest on loans to upgrade is allowable).

 If you let only part of a property, such as the top floor of a three-storey house, you can deduct expenses only for the part you are letting.

Do not include in this calculation the interest on any loans you have taken out to buy or improve the property you are letting. It can, however, be included in your tax return as an outgoing.

If you own property jointly (such as with your partner), you should mark the calculation JOINT and divide the rental income between the co-owners. Normally you will divide the letting income equally, but if one of the co-owners does not pay tax, or pays tax at a lower rate, then an unequal division of income may save tax. If you think this applies to you, seek expert advice, such as from an accountant.

You may – especially if your rental income is more than £15,000 a year – find yourself being charged tax on rent arrears, that is, rents which have become payable but which you have not received. If you never get the rent, you can claim bad debt relief, but you are out of pocket in the meantime.

This sounds monstrous until you accept that the Inland Revenue has its own way of doing things, which means that you include all income *earned* in the tax year even *if you have never seen a penny of it*. This is known as the 'earnings basis' of taxation.

The alternative – available to most (not all) people whose gross rental income does not exceed £15,000 – is known as the 'cash basis' – that is, what you actually receive in rent and pay in expenses. What you can't do, however, is switch to-and-fro between the two to suit yourself.

For further information see the Inland Revenue leaflet IR150 *Taxation of Rents*.

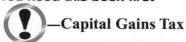

—Capital Gains Tax

Capital gains tax is a tax you have to pay if you sell property at a profit. While your own home is generally exempt from capital gains tax, property that is let is usually taxable.

Detailed advice about capital gains tax is, however, outside the scope of this book. You must seek expert advice – see an accountant.

A note on Stamp Duty

Most people associate stamp duty with house purchase, but in fact it is in origin a tax on legal documents – including tenancy agreements. The reason for paying Stamp Duty in your case is that you will need to have done so in order to produce your tenancy agreement as evidence in court.

Picture the scene. A landlord has taken a tenant to court. It is an open and shut case. The landlord produces the tenancy agreement in court – and tenant's lawyer objects. 'This tenancy agreement is not admissible as evidence, because it has not been stamped'. Collapse of landlord's case.

Legal lore

This goes back to the Stamp Act 1891, which stated that a document relating to property 'shall not be given in evidence, or available for any purpose whatever, unless it is duly stamped in accordance with the law in force at the time it was executed'. This includes lease and tenancy agreements.

As in everything else, there are exceptions. The rules do not apply in criminal proceedings, for example. The law (the Stamp Act 1891 – see above) also gives the judge a duty to note 'any insufficiency of stamp' and allow this to be put right, on the spot if possible, whereupon the document can be used in evidence.

Judges don't come into court armed with stamp duty leaflets and petty cash boxes, and it is up to you to make sure that your tenancy agreement is stamped if it needs to be.

Here are the rules at the time of writing. The mantra is '£5,000'.

- An assured shorthold tenancy *does not* require stamp duty if the annual rent *is less than* £5,000 and the tenancy was granted after 28 March 2000;
- An assured shorthold tenancy *does* require stamp duty if the annual rent is more than £5,000.

Remember that the tax is on the document – and the main burden of tax falls on the copy of the tenancy

agreement signed by you and handed over to the tenant.
The tax on this is not your responsibility. All you have
to pay is £5 on the copy of the tenancy agreement
signed by the tenant and (hopefully!) in your file.

For details of stamp duty payable by tenants and the
interest and penalties for late payment, access
>http://inlandrevenue.gov.uk< and type 'stamp duty' in
their search box.

If your transaction attracts stamp duty, you must pay up
within 30 days of the date of your agreement. If you are
late paying, the taxman can penalise you for late
presentation of your document. The penalty clocks up
like a taxi fare meter.

—It makes a lot of sense, if you have not paid stamp duty
and need to use your tenancy agreement in court, to pay
up and get the document stamped before you start
proceedings.

How to pay up

Send to the Inland Revenue (see page 163):

- the copy of the agreement signed by the tenant (keep
  a photocopy for your file);
- a cheque for the amount due, made payable to Inland
  Revenue Only – Stamp Duties;
- a stamped addressed envelope addressed to yourself.

The assured shorthold tenancy agreement

You can download this agreement from the website. You will need two copies, one marked *Original* and the other marked *Duplicate*. You will sign the original and give it to the tenant to keep. The tenant will sign the duplicate and return it to you to keep. See *The nitty gritty* on page 93.

A note on the Standard Letting Provisions

Most tenancy agreements print the Standard Letting Provisions in very small print on the back of the tenancy agreement, usually in very pale ink. We have not only printed them out full size; we have also added an explanation. You may like to give a copy of our explanation to your tenant.

First, however, the agreements. Study our worked example before putting your own agreement together.

Original (landlord to sign, tenant to keep)

Agreement for an Assured Shorthold Tenancy

Date: 1 September 2001

THE LANDLORD: William Shakespeare

ADDRESS: New Place, Stratford upon Avon, Warwickshire

THE TENANT: Kit Marlowe

THE PROPERTY: 2 Gentlemen's Walk, Verona Street, Stratford upon Avon

THE CONTENTS: The items at the Property specified in the inventory attached to this agreement, and signed by the Landlord and Tenant.

START DATE: 1 September 2001

INITIAL PERIOD: six months from the start date. After the initial period, if the letting continues, it does so as a periodic letting. The period is a calendar month, and the first day of each period is the same day of the month as the start date.

RENT: £350.00 per calendar month for the duration of the letting.

PAYABLE: monthly in advance. The Tenant is to make the first payment on the signing of this agreement, and subsequent payments on the same day of the month as the start date.

DEPOSIT: £350.00 to be paid to the Landlord on the signing of this agreement.

A The Landlord lets and the Tenant takes the Property for the initial period on the terms of this agreement which incorporates the Standard Letting Provisions.

B.1 The Landlord can end the letting on the last day of the initial period, or after the initial period, by service of the Landlord's notice of intention to seek possession.

B.2 The Tenant can end the letting by vacating the Property on the last day of the initial period, or after that by giving the Landlord one month's written notice.

C The Tenant acknowledges that this agreement creates an Assured Shorthold Tenancy.

D The Landlord's address for service of notices (including notices of proceedings) is the address given for the Landlord at the start of this agreement.

E The Landlord and the Tenant have agreed the following variations (if any) of the Standard Letting Provisions:

The Tenant may keep his cat, Prospero, at the Property.

SIGNED by the Landlord William Shakespeare

Duplicate (tenant(s) to sign, landlord to keep)

Agreement for an Assured Shorthold Tenancy

Date: 1 September 2001

THE LANDLORD: William Shakespeare

ADDRESS: New Place, Stratford upon Avon, Warwickshire

THE TENANT: Kit Marlowe

THE PROPERTY: 2 Gentlemen's Walk, Verona Street, Stratford upon Avon

THE CONTENTS: The items at the Property specified in the inventory attached to this agreement, and signed by the Landlord and Tenant.

START DATE: 1 September 2001

INITIAL PERIOD: six months from the start date. After the initial period, if the letting continues, it does so as a periodic letting. The period is a calendar month, and the first day of each period is the same day of the month as the start date.

RENT: £350.00 per calendar month for the duration of the letting.

PAYABLE: monthly in advance. The Tenant is to make the first payment on the signing of this agreement, and subsequent payments on the same day of the month as the start date.

DEPOSIT: £350.00 to be paid to the Landlord on the signing of this agreement.

A The Landlord lets and the Tenant takes the Property for the initial period on the terms of this agreement which incorporates the Standard Letting Provisions.

B.1 The Landlord can end the letting on the last day of the initial period, or after the initial period, by service of the Landlord's notice of intention to seek possession.

B.2 The Tenant can end the letting by vacating the Property on the last day of the initial period, or after that by giving the Landlord one month's written notice.

C The Tenant acknowledges that this agreement creates an Assured Shorthold Tenancy.

D The Landlord's address for service of notices (including notices of proceedings) is the address given for the Landlord at the start of this agreement.

E The Landlord and the Tenant have agreed the following variations (if any) of the Standard Letting Provisions:

The Tenant may keep his cat, Prospero, at the Property.

SIGNED by the Tenant

Kit Marlowe

Standard Letting Provisions

1.1 'The Landlord' means the Landlord named in the tenancy agreement and includes whoever owns the interest in the Property which gives the right to possession of it when the tenancy ends.

1.2 Whenever there is more than one tenant, the full extent of their obligations can be enforced against all of them jointly and against each of them individually.

1.3 A right given to the Landlord to enter the Property extends to anyone the Landlord authorises to enter (including the Landlord's agent and/or surveyor), and includes the right to bring workmen and appliances onto the Property for a stated purpose.

1.4 The singular includes the plural and vice versa; and the generic plural (they/their) is used both for masculine (he/his) and feminine singular (she/her).

1.5 'The Property' includes any part or parts of the Property and, if the context requires, the Contents.

1.6 'The Deposit' includes all or part of it, as the context requires, and also interest earned on it.

2 THE TENANT IS TO:

2.1 Pay the Rent at the time and in the manner stated in the agreement without any deduction, and by standing order if so requested by the Landlord.

2.2 Arrange immediately with the relevant supply company for all accounts for gas, electricity and telephone (if any) at the Property to be addressed to the Tenant in their own name and pay all standing charges for these and all charges for gas and electricity supplied to the Property and for telephone calls made from the Property during the letting period.

2.3 Pay the Council Tax and water rates for the Property applicable to the letting period.

2.4 Use the Property as a private residence for occupation by the named Tenant(s), and, if the Landlord has so agreed, by the named Tenant's children under 18.

2.5 Keep the Property clean and tidy and the interior of the Property in good decorative condition, and at least up to the standard existing on the start date.

2.6 Keep the drains, drainage system and gutters free from obstruction.

2.7 Replace broken glass in the windows if the breakage is the Tenant's fault.

2.8 Notify the Landlord promptly of any defect or disrepair – especially anything that compromises health and safety – in any of the following:

● the structure of the property;
● the exterior of the property;
● installations for the supply of water, gas, oil, electricity, sanitation (including basins, sinks, bath and WCs);
● installations and appliances for space heating and water heating;
● other gas or electrical appliances.

To comply with this obligation, the Tenant can inform the Landlord in person or by telephone, letter, e-mail or fax. Where the Tenant informs the Landlord orally, they should confirm this in writing.

2.9 Notify the Landlord promptly (where the Property is part of a larger building, such as a flat in a block) of any defect or disrepair in the block which adversely affects the Tenant's use of the Property (see 2.8 above for methods of notification).

2.10 Permit the Landlord at reasonable times to enter the Property:

- to inspect the condition of the Property and the Contents;
- to carry out gas and electrical safety checks;
- to carry out repairs for which the Landlord is responsible.

If there is any damage or disrepair for which the Tenant is responsible, or if any of the Contents are missing, the Landlord may serve on the Tenant a notice in writing specifying any repairs and/or replacements which are necessary and requiring the Tenant to carry them out. If the Tenant does not do so within 28 days after receiving the Landlord's notice, the Tenant is to permit the Landlord to enter the Property, so that the Landlord can carry out the repairs and/or replacements. The full cost to the Landlord of doing this is to be a debt due from the Tenant to the Landlord, which the Tenant will pay immediately.

2.11 Keep the Contents clean, and equipment and/or appliances at the Property in good working order.

2.12 Keep the garden (if any) of the Property clean, tidy and properly tended, the grass cut and any hedges that belong to the Property at a reasonable height and width.

2.13 Arrange for chimneys to be swept regularly.

2.14 Arrange that at all times during the tenancy there is a valid television licence in force for any television set(s) at the Property, and pay the licence fee.

2.15 Pay in full the Landlord's costs, including legal costs, resulting from any breach by the Tenant of any obligation contained in this agreement, including costs of

- repairing damage and disrepair for which the Tenant is responsible under this lease;
- recovering money from the Tenant, including rent arrears and bank charges for re-presenting cheques.

2.16 Comply (where the property is a leasehold dwelling) with the rules which regulate the use of the Property and the conduct of its occupiers.

2.17 Remove any rubbish and return the Property and the Contents to the Landlord at the end of the tenancy clean, tidy and in accordance with the provisions of this agreement. If the Landlord asks, the Tenant is to allow the Landlord access to the Property for the purpose of checking the inventory at the end of the tenancy.

2.18 Prevent infringement of the restrictions in clause 3 below by anyone living in or visiting the Property, or any animal at the Property.

3 THE TENANT IS NOT TO:

3.1 Interfere with or make any alteration to the structure of the Property or (if applicable) the layout of the garden.

3.2 Sell, charge, hire out or remove the Contents from the Property.

3.3 Deface or damage the Property or the Contents (including by use of nails, hooks, screws and adhesives).

3.4 Be guilty of conduct that is a nuisance to neighbours. In particular the Tenant is not to

3.4.1 make any noise that is audible outside the Property from 11 p.m. to 8 a.m. daily;

3.4.2 be guilty of harassment or abuse on grounds of race, sex, sexual orientation or disability.

3.5 Keep animals at the Property, except with the Landlord's prior written permission.

3.6 Do anything that gives the insurers of the Property and the Contents any reason to

● refuse payment; or

● increase the premiums.

3.7 Leave the Property vacant for more than 28 consecutive days without warning the Landlord in writing before doing so.

3.8 Keep any dangerous or inflammable substance on the Property, including any garage, shed, outbuilding or parking space within the boundaries of the Property.

3.9 Sublet the Property, take in lodgers or paying guests or share or part with possession of the Property, or transfer the benefit of this agreement.

3.10 Cut down or remove trees, bushes, shrubs or plants in the garden without the Landlord's prior consent.

3.11 Use any garage, outbuilding or parking space within the boundaries of the Property to park any vehicle other than a roadworthy private vehicle.

4 If any rent or other money payable by the Tenant to the Landlord under this agreement is not paid within 14 days of the date it becomes due, interest on it is payable at 5% per annum above bank base rate, calculated on a day to day basis from the due date until it is paid, and the interest is to be compounded every 3 months.

5.1 The Landlord holds the Deposit as security for compliance by the Tenant with the terms of this agreement. If the Tenant fails to comply and as a result the Landlord suffers loss the Landlord may take an amount – which is not to exceed the loss – from the deposit.

5.2 The Landlord is to keep the Deposit in an interest-bearing bank or building society account, separate from the Landlord's own money until *either*

- the Landlord takes it for a reason which this agreement permits; *or*
- the Landlord returns it to the Tenant.

5.3 If the Landlord has recourse to the Deposit during the tenancy, the Landlord may immediately demand from the Tenant whatever amount is required to restore the amount of the Deposit to the original sum.

5.4 The Deposit, plus interest (net of tax) earned on it, is to be paid to the Tenant at the termination of the Tenancy less the following:

5.4.1 Such amount as the Landlord takes as compensation for loss in accordance with 5.1, *and*

5.4.2 The cost to the Landlord of cleaning the Property and Contents (including carpets, curtains and other soft furnishings) when the tenancy ends.

5.5 If the Deposit is not enough to cover these costs, the Tenant is to pay the Landlord on demand such further amount as the Landlord needs for the purpose.

6 SUBJECT TO CLAUSES 7 AND 8 BELOW, THE LANDLORD IS TO:

6.1 Comply with the obligations under Section 11 of the Landlord and Tenant Act 1985,

- to keep the structure and exterior of the Property in repair;
- to keep in repair and in proper working order the installations in the Property for the supply of water, gas, electricity and sanitation and to ensure that the Property has a current gas safety certificate;
- to keep in repair and proper working order the installations in the Property for space heating and water heating.

6.2 Comply with the obligation under the Gas Safety (Installation and Use) Regulations 1998 to have all gas appliances, flues and other fittings checked annually to make sure they are safe and working satisfactorily.

6.3 Comply with the obligations under the Electrical Equipment (Safety) Regulations 1994 to ensure the safety of electrical appliances at the Property.

6.4 Comply with the obligation under the Furniture and Furnishings (Fire) (Safety) Regulations 1988 to ensure that all of the Landlord's upholstered furniture, as well as beds, headboards, mattresses, sofa beds, futons, cushions and pillows, meet fire safety standards.

7 Unless there is a threat to human safety, the obligations on the Landlord at clause 6.1 do not apply until the Tenant notifies the Landlord of the defect or disrepair. The Landlord's obligations do not extend beyond those imposed by statute, and are to be interpreted as such.

8 The Landlord does not have to carry out work which has become necessary because of the Tenant's breach of their obligations.

9 If the Landlord or the Landlord's mortgage lender is entitled to repossess the Property on either Ground 2 (mortgage arrears) or Ground 8 (substantial rent arrears) Schedule 2 Part 1 Housing Act 1988, the tenancy automatically comes to an end upon the making of a court order for possession on those grounds, even if the order is made during any fixed period of the tenancy.

Notes on Standard Letting Provisions

We have prepared these notes to clarify the Standard Letting Provisions. We suggest you give your tenant a copy.

1.1 This definition of the landlord means that if you sell your property, or if you die, your rights as landlord under the agreement will be handed on to any new owner of the property.

1.2 Each named tenant is liable to you for the full amount of the rent, which is why it is important to list all tenants' names in your forms. This means that if there are rent arrears, no joint tenant can weasel out by claiming to have paid their share of the rent.

1.3 You have a right to enter the property, and so has anyone else on your say-so. This enables you to send in workmen if necessary.

1.4 We have opted for the generic plural ('your tenant must pay their rent') instead of 'he/she/it/him; ... etc. If it bothers you, we apologise.

The tenant is to:

2.1 If you want the rent paid by standing order, you can insist on this.

2.2 and 2.3 Our agreement assumes that the tenant will pay the Council Tax, gas, water, electricity and telephone bills. If you want to make other arrangements, you need to add the following words to Clause E of the tenancy agreement: 'The Landlord is to pay [Council Tax/water charges for the Property] [charges for oil/gas/electricity supplied to the Property]'.

If your property is a flat, you may well pay a ground rent and service charge to the owner of the building. The standard letting provisions assume that you will continue to pay these and that the level of rent you charge will allow you to recoup these costs. You can in theory make your tenant pay the ground rent and service charge, but remember that these costs are your responsibility and if your tenant defaults the owner of the building will blame you.

2.4 This prevents the tenant using the property as anything other than a private home.

2.5 This should be straightforward. The tenant does not have to improve the interior of your property, but they must keep it in the condition in which they took it over.

2.6 'Drains' includes septic tanks. If you have a septic tank it is sensible to make sure your tenant understands the workings and the needs of this form of drainage.

2.7 Crystal clear (geddit?).

2.8 You as landlord are responsible for the repair and safety of the structure, exterior, gas and electrical installations, etc. But what happens if something goes wrong and you don't know about it? The purpose of this clause is to oblige the tenant to tell you.

2.9 This clause applies to flats, where of course a problem with one can affect the others.

2.10 This clause gives you the right to inspect the property. You can ask the tenant in writing to carry out any necessary repairs or replacements for which they are responsible. If they refuse to do so, you can carry out the work yourself and charge your expenses to them. In practice, you may want to deduct these expenses from the deposit.

2.11 This of course applies only if there are 'contents', appliances, etc, to consider.

2.12 This clause of course applies only if there is a garden. Where applicable, it guards against thigh-high grass and 20-foot leylandii hedges.

2.13 Unswept chimneys are a major fire hazard, and insurance companies may refuse to pay out after a chimney fire if the chimney has been neglected.

2.14 The tenant buys his or her own television licence.

2.15 This clause makes the tenant liable – in theory at least – for your costs if they do not keep their side of the bargain – including paying your bank charges if any cheques bounce.

2.16 This clause makes your tenant responsible for complying with the rules by which you yourself, as leaseholder, have to abide.

2.17 Straightforward – they hand over the property in good order. This clause also provides for an inventory check at the end of the tenancy.

2.18 If any damage is done, this prevents the tenant blaming it on anyone else.

The tenant is not to:

3.1 No extensions, no re-siting of flower beds, no tree-felling ...

3.2 The tenant may not sell your sofa, donate your dresser or loan out your lawnmower.

3.3 This stops the tenant putting up shelves, hammering picture hooks into the walls or even sticking up posters. Many landlords say 'Put up your pictures, but make good before you leave'.

3.4 The tenant must not annoy or harass the neighbours. This covers everything from name calling to having a late-night band practice. This type of obligation is notoriously difficult to enforce; but you can't say we didn't try.

3.5 You can use your discretion here – how fond are you of animals and how easy-going are the neighbours?

3.6 This prevents your tenant from doing anything on your property that would adversely affect the insurance.

3.7 If the property is empty for more than 28 days you may find that your buildings and contents insurance policy will lapse.

3.8 No bombs, shotguns, chemistry sets or portable Calor gas heaters in the house, garage, greenhouse, garden shed or parking areas.

3.9 This restriction means that the named tenants cannot sublet your property or allow anyone else to live there. This clause does not stop the tenant from having visitors occasionally.

3.10 This protects your trees, bushes and shrubs and prevents the tenant from getting the Ground Force team in.

3.11 This protects you against the parking of commercial vehicles and also the parking or dumping of dead and decaying vehicles on the property.

4 This allows you to charge high interest on unpaid or overdue rent.

5.1 This allows you to take the deposit if the tenant breaks the rules and this causes you loss.

5.2 You must hold the deposit in an interest-bearing account, separate from your own money.

5.3 If you need to use part of the deposit, this clause enables you to make the tenant top it up again.

5.4 At the end of the tenancy the tenant gets the deposit back, less

> 5.4.1 any of it needed to put right anything the tenant has done or failed to do

> 5.4.2 the cost of cleaning carpets, upholstery, etc (if any) at the end of the tenancy.

5.5 If the deposit is not enough to put things right, you can make the tenant pay the difference.

6 This clause spells out your statutory obligations for repairs, health and safety. We have put them in here because you cannot exclude them anyway. For fuller details of these obligations, refer to pages 32–42.

7 You are always responsible for disrepair which is a threat to health and safety – whether or not anyone has told you about it. This obligation is imposed by the Defective Premises Act 1972. Apart from the health and safety obligations, you are not responsible for any defects or disrepair unless and until the tenant tells you about them.

8 You do not have to carry out work which has become necessary through the tenant's fault.

9 This clause replaces what used to be called the forfeiture clause – by which a landlord could simply kick the tenant out if they broke the tenancy agreement. The forfeiture clause is no longer appropriate for residential lettings, since the landlord needs a court order for possession anyway. The purpose of our new clause is to end the contractual tenancy if the court orders that the landlord should have the property back. It also protects the landlord's mortgage lender – an important provision in buy-to-let situations.

Your inventory

Your inventory is a room-by-room record of the contents of the property. Our sample concerns a one-bedroom flat that has been fully furnished and comprehensively equipped.

Remember to state the decorative condition of the accommodation, from 'newly decorated' through 'very good' to 'poor' and to add wording such as 'all items new or in very good condition unless otherwise stated'. Your inventory should draw attention to anything that is shabby or damaged, so that nobody can blame the damage on your tenant.

1. If you are a keen photographer, or own a camcorder, you may like to photograph the property room by room. Landlords have been known to win court cases because they were able to provide evidence of the 'before' as well as the 'after'!

2. Always specify the manufacturer of major items. Tenants have been known to swap the microwave for an inferior model and take away the expensive one.

3. Always check electrical appliances before putting them on the inventory. If it doesn't work reliably, you must repair or replace it.

4. Always provide instruction manuals and include them in the inventory. If you have lost the instructions for something, it is worth contacting the manufacturer and asking for a fresh copy.

The inventory should be signed by you and by your tenant after you have checked through it together.

Any changes of contents made during the tenancy should be added to, or deleted from, both the landlord's and the tenant's Inventories. The checklist below is for your guidance only. You will of course want to produce your own. When you are happy with your inventory, print out two copies, one for you and one for your tenant. One should be attached to the original tenancy agreement, the other to the duplicate.

Inventory

All items new or in very good condition unless otherwise stated

Kitchen

Newly decorated

[*Vinyl*] flooring

[ ] light fittings

[*Slate grey*] worktops

[ ] window blind

1 [*Zanussi*][washer/dryer] model no [ ]

Instructions for same

1 sink unit with stainless steel sink

1 [*Philips*] [*electric*] cooker model no [ ]

Instructions for same

1 [*Smeg*] electric cooker hood model no [   ]

Instructions for same

1 [*Whirlpool*] fridge-freezer model no [   ]

Instructions for same

1 [*Matsui*] microwave cooker [with oven, grill and defrosting facilities] model no [   ]

Instructions for same

1 [*Morphy Richards*] electric kettle model no [   ]

Instructions for same

[   ] wall cupboards

[   ] low cupboards

[   ] drawer units containing

(here you fill in any cutlery, crockery, cooking utensils, etc that you provide)

1 table

[ ] chairs

1 waste bin

1 [*Hoover upright*] vacuum cleaner model no [ ] with tools

Instructions for same

1 packet spare vacuum cleaner bags

[ ] dusters

1 squeegee mop

1 bucket

1 dustpan and brush

Always give tenants the means to be houseproud; you ——— never know your luck.

Bathroom

Newly decorated

[*Vinyl*] flooring

1 [*pendant*] light fitting with shade

You need this book first

> 1 strip light over wash basin
>
> 1 bath with [*Mira*] power shower
>
> Instructions for same
>
> 1 [*non-slip rubber*] bathmat
>
> 1 shower curtain and rail
>
> 1 lavatory [with *pine* seat]
>
> 1 wash basin
>
> 1 mirror
>
> 1 waste paper bin
>
> 1 toilet roll holder
>
> 1 lavatory brush
>
> 1 shelf
>
> 1 linen bin
>
> 1 wall heater
>
> 1 soap dish
>
> 1 extractor fan

Airing cupboard

Slatted shelves

Tank with thick insulated jacket

Controls for storage heaters

Immersion heater

Controls for same

Instructions for same

Living room

Newly decorated

1 fitted carpet

1 pendant light fitting with shade

1 [*metal action*] sofa bed

1 [*Flokati*] rug

[ ] scatter cushions

[ ] pairs of [*Sanderson Country Trail cotton*] curtains
[+ *matching tie backs*]

You need this book first

1 dining table

[ ] dining chairs [*with Sanderson Country Trail cotton seat cushions*]

[ ] bookcases

1 desk

1 table lamp

1 typist's chair

1 coffee table

[ ] armchairs

1 [*Philips*] television and stand model no [ ]

Instructions for same

[ ] chests of drawers

1 waste paper bin

1 [electric storage] heater

Instructions for same

[ ] pictures

Bedroom

Newly decorated

1 pendant light with shade

Fitted carpet

1 double bed with headboard and drawers under

1 fitted wardrobe with shelves

1 dressing table

1 chest of drawers

2 bedside tables

2 bedside lamps

1 [*electric storage*] heater

Instructions for same

We have thoroughly checked this inventory and agree
that all is as set out above.

Signed.................................. Tenant

Signed.................................. Landlord

..............................date

Sample letters and other documents

Below you will find worked examples of:

1. Letter to insurance company.

2. Reference request.

3. Demand for rent.

4. Receipt for rent.

5. Receipt for deposit.

You can use the model letters on the website, topping and tailing them to suit your needs.

1. Letter to insurance company

Daffodil Cottage
Keswick
Cumbria

Date: 2 October 2001

To: The Stardust Insurance Company
Stargazers Lane
London EC1

From William Wordsworth

Dear Sirs

*Policy No: WW/212/SGP/890/2 Daffodil Cottage
Keswick Cumbria*

I have Daffodil Cottage and its contents insured with
you under the above policy.

I am intending to let the property [including the
contents].

Will you please confirm that my insurance will continue during the letting, and that I will be fully insured in the event of:

- the injury or death of my tenant, their family or visitors, for which I am legally liable;

- damage to the property and/or its contents by my tenant, their family or visitors,

- theft of contents by my tenant, their family or visitors,

- damage to my tenants' property caused by disrepair or defects in my property and/or its contents.

I would be grateful for your early reply and thank you in anticipation of your kind assistance.

Yours faithfully,

William Wordsworth

2. Reference request

Daffodil Cottage
Keswick
Cumbria
15 October 2001

Mr P B Shelley
12 Skylark Rise
Crawley
Surrey

Dear Sir,

I am considering letting a house to Mr Leigh Hunt, who has given your name as a referee. I should be grateful if you would kindly tell me how long you have known Mr Hunt and in what capacity; and let me have your views on his suitability as a tenant, including his ability to pay the rent and to keep the property in good order.

I thank you in anticipation of your help in this matter and attach a stamped addressed envelope for your reply.

Yours faithfully,

William Wordsworth

3. Rent demand

Date: 1 November 2001

Landlord: John Keats

Landlord's address *

> The Old Muse
>
> Moorgate
>
> London EC2

[*DO NOT FORGET LANDLORD'S ADDRESS – it is not legal without it!*]

Property address:

> Endymion House
>
> Nightingale Way
>
> St Agnes, Cornwall

Tenant: Samuel Taylor Coleridge

Amount: £400

Period of Letting: 1 November to 30 November 2001

Please make immediate payment of the rent for the stated period of letting. Thank you.

....

Landlord's signature,

John Keats

4. Receipt for rent

Date: 1 November 2001

Landlord: John Keats

Property address:
Endymion House
Nightingale Way
St Agnes, Cornwall

Tenant: Samuel Taylor Coleridge

Amount: £400

Period of Letting: 1 November to 30 November 2001

I acknowledge receipt of the rent for the stated period of letting.

John Keats

Landlord's Signature

5. Receipt for deposit

Date: 1 November 2001

Landlord: John Keats

Property address: Endymion House, Nightingale Way, St Agnes, Cornwall.

Tenant: Samuel Taylor Coleridge

Amount of deposit: £400

I acknowledge receipt of your deposit which I agree to hold on the terms of the Tenancy Agreement between us of today's date.

John Keats

Landlord's signature

Sample Notice of Landlord's Intention to Seek Possession

HOUSING ACT 1988

Sections 21 (1) (b) and 21 (4) (a)

Notice of Landlord's Intention to Seek Possession

To: Samuel Taylor Coleridge

Of: Endymion House, Nightingale Way, St Agnes, Cornwall

From: John Keats

Of: The Old Muse, Moorgate, London EC2

Property: Endymion House, Nightingale Way, St Agnes, Cornwall

Possession date: 31 December 2001

I give you notice that I require possession of the property on the possession date.

Date: 25 October 2001

Signed: John Keats

I/We acknowledge receipt of the original notice, of which this is a copy

Signed: Sam Coleridge

Your address list

You may like to staple this list to the inner cover of your file. Add and update as you go. If you are a serial landlord, do one per property. It could save a lot of trawling through directories.

Council

Property reference number.............................
Telephone number
Council Tax
Environmental Services
Housing Benefit
Fax number
E-mail details
Contact names

Water

Reference number
Telephone number
Fax number
Contact names

Electricity

Reference number
Telephone number
Meter reading
Bills
Fax number
Contact names

Gas

Reference number
Telephone number
Meter readings
Bills
Fax number
Contact names

Plumber

Name
Telephone number

Electrician

Name
Telephone number

Builder

Name
Telephone number

Useful Contacts

Association of Residential Letting Agents (ARLA)

Maple House

53–55 Woodside Road

Amersham HP6 6AA

Telephone 01923 896555

Website: www.arla.co.uk

Details of buy-to-let schemes, local ARLA members and free booklet, *Trouble Free Letting* – send them a stamped addressed envelope for your copy or download from the website.

Buy-to-let hotline 01923 896555

Gas safety

To find your local CORGI fitter call 01256 372300.

Health and Safety Executive Gas Safety Action Line for tenants and landlords: 0800 300 363

Website: www.corgi-gas.com

Electrical Installation and Safety Certificates

National Inspection Council for Electrical Installations

Telephone 020 7564 2323

Website: www.niceic.org.uk

Home Energy Efficiency Scheme (HEES)

A Government funded scheme to improve heating, energy efficiency and insulation, at no charge to landlords, in rented property whose tenants are disabled and/or on benefits.

Telephone 0800 952 1555

Small Landlords' Association

78 Tachbrook Street

London SW1V 2NA

Telephone 0870 241 0471

Website: http://www.landlords.org.uk

The vast majority of landlords are 'small' – over 90% let just one property – and the SLA is their 'voice' and a valuable source of free advice and assistance and useful leaflets. Membership is currently £55 a year and you can get tax relief on this.

For advice on the SLA's insurance scheme contact Hamilton Fraser: 020 8440 8338

Incorporated Association of Landlords

'The professional body for private landlords'

You can join online at http://www.ial.org.uk

Advice on buy-to-let

ARLA has a leaflet on its website: access
http://arla.co.uk/whatisbuyandlet.htm

Access *Your Mortgage Magazine* (Financial Website of
the Year) at http://www.yourmortgage.co.uk

Trading Standards

Advice on many aspects of letting your property,
including electrical safety, upholstered furniture and
much more. Look in your local telephone directory
under Trading Standards or access the website, the
Trading Standards Net at
http://www.tradingstandards.net

Stamp Duty

Worthing Stamp Office

Room 35

East Block

Barrington Road

Worthing BN12 4XJ

Telephone 01903 508962

Customer Service Manager: 01903 509957

DTLR

The Department for Transport, Local Government and

the Regions offers a wealth of helpful information for landlords and tenants.

DTLR Free Literature,
PO Box No. 236,
Wetherby
LS23 7NB
Telephone 0870 1226 236,
Fax 0870 1226 237
Websites: www.dtlr.gov.uk and
http://www.housing.detr.gov.uk

DTI Booklets

Several useful publications are available; and they are particularly sound on furniture and fire safety.

DTI Publications Order Line
Admail 528
London SW1W 8YT
Telephone 0870 1502 500

Legal Answers

'This FREE service enables you to search for answers to legal problems'. There is a useful section on assured shorthold tenancies. Access: http://www.legalhelp.co.uk

Law Solutions

This website offers a great deal of free legal information, including a section called *Information for Landlords*. Access: http://lawsolutions.co.uk

Inland Revenue

There are several leaflets available, all in clear English. Try IR87 *Letting and Your Home,* IP150 *Taxation of Rents. A guide to property income* and IP283 *Helpsheet, Private Residence Relief.* You can download leaflets from the Inland Revenue website at www.inlandrevenue.gov.uk

or call its orderline on 08459 000 404, 8 a.m. to 10 p.m, seven days a week (when that office is closed, call 08459 000444, or e-mail: saorderline.ir@gtnet.gov.uk)

For advice on your particular situation, look under Inland Revenue in your local telephone directory.

Checking creditworthiness

The Register of County Court Judgments, maintained by Registry Trust Ltd
173–175 Cleveland Street
London W1P 5PE
Telephone 020 7380 0133.

For £4.50 a name (make out the cheque to Registry Trust Limited) you can get a printout of any judgments made against that name.

The Individual Insolvency Register came into operation in March 1999 and keeps details of bankruptcy and individual voluntary arrangements (a sort of half-way house between solvency and insolvency). You can apply free of charge:

> *in person* at any official receiver's office (listed in your local telephone directory), where you fill in a form and receive a printout of the information.

> *in writing* to

> The Insolvency Service
> 5th Floor, West Wing
> 45–46 Stephenson Street
> Birmingham B2 4UP.

> *by telephone* to the Insolvency Service on 020 7637 1110 and they will tell you over the phone whether an individual is bankrupt (or is subject to bankruptcy proceedings) or has entered into an IVA.

Index

Printed in the United Kingdom by The Stationery Office Ltd, London
TJ5583   C20   11/01   659437   19585